Your Towns and C

Castle Point
in the Great War

Your Towns and Cities in the Great War

Castle Point
in the Great War

Ken Porter and Stephen Wynn

Pen & Sword
MILITARY

First published in Great Britain in 2015 by
PEN & SWORD MILITARY
an imprint of
Pen and Sword Books Ltd
47 Church Street
Barnsley
South Yorkshire S70 2AS

ISBN 978 1 47382 311 2

Printed and bound in England
by CPI Group (UK) Ltd, Croydon, CR0 4YY

Typeset in Times New Roman by Chic Graphics

Pen & Sword Books Ltd incorporates the imprints of
Pen & Sword Archaeology, Atlas, Aviation, Battleground, Discovery,
Family History, History, Maritime, Military, Naval, Politics, Railways,
Select, Social History, Transport, True Crime, Claymore Press,
Frontline Books, Leo Cooper, Praetorian Press, Remember When,
Seaforth Publishing and Wharncliffe.

For a complete list of Pen and Sword titles please contact
Pen and Sword Books Limited
47 Church Street, Barnsley, South Yorkshire, S70 2AS, England
E-mail: enquiries@pen-and-sword.co.uk
Website: www.pen-and-sword.co.uk

Contents

Author Biographies

Ken Porter was born in Laindon in 1944; his passions have always been sport and history. At school he took an active part in athletics and football, then in his early teens cricket took over and became his life's passion.

Ken is a leading enthusiast in the Basildon Heritage Group and Laindon and District Community Archive and he gives talks to local societies, which are always well attended. His enthusiasm for history inspires others to get involved and share their memories. Ken's interest in the 1914-1918 period stems from the discovery of his maternal grandfather James Frederick Pitts' involvement in the Great War.

Stephen Wynn has just retired from the Police Force, having served with Essex Police as a Constable for thirty years. His interest in history has been fuelled by the fact that both his grandfathers served in and survived the First World War, (one with the Royal Irish Rifles, the other in the Merchant Navy), and his father was a member of the Royal Army Ordnance Corps during the Second World War.

His sons, Luke and Ross, were also members of the armed forces, serving five tours of Afghanistan between 2008 and 2013. Both were injured and this experience led to his first book, *Two Sons in a War Zone – Afghanistan: The True Story of a Father's Conflict,* which was published in 2010. He has also written three crime thrillers.

Ken and Stephen have collaborated on a previous book, published in 2012, *German P.O.W. Camp 266 – Langdon Hills,* which became a number one bestseller in Basildon Waterstones.

Acknowledgements

Writing a book of this nature requires a considerable amount of research, and we could not have completed it without the help and co-operation of a large number of people and interested groups. We would like to express our appreciation to those who helped us to verify information that we sourced, including: members of the Basildon Heritage, Laindon and District Community Archive; Canvey Island Community Archive; Benfleet Community Archive; Hadleigh Community Archive; Canvey Bay Museum.

Then there are the individuals who have provided information and made photographs available: Phil Coley, Ronnie Pigram, Graham Cook, Janet Penn, Val Jackson, Len Hawkins, Jo Cullen, Sue Ranford, Denise Rowling, John and Ann Rugg and Martin Stibbard.

Every effort has been made to contact the copyright holders of the images and documents we have used in compiling this book. We would appreciate any additional information, which can be passed on to us through the publisher.

Ken Porter and Stephen Wynn, 2014

Introduction

The Borough of Castle Point includes the old ecclesiastical parishes of South Benfleet, Canvey Island, Hadleigh and Thundersley, but back in 1914, on the outbreak of the First World War, Castle Point did not exist.

From Saxon times up until 1834, the manors of Thundersley and South Benfleet were part of the Barstable Hundred. Canvey Island was also part of the Barstable Hundred, although responsibility for it was split between a number of the nearby parishes. Hadleigh was part of the Rochford Hundred. A hundred is a term derived from Saxon land holdings, in which a 'hide' was an area of land considered capable of supporting up to fifty people. The 'hundred' was a larger administrative area of one hundred hides, which possessed the authority to settle its own local disputes. In time it became a subdivision of a county or shire.

In 1926 Canvey Island gained its own local authority, the Canvey Island Urban District. Three years later, when the Benfleet Urban District Council was formed, it included the parishes of Hadleigh, Thundersley and South Benfleet. A district guide produced at the time stated that:

> *The formation of these urban areas west of Southend-on-Sea was due to the very rapid development following the Great War, a development which is bound to continue and which rightly directed, with due regard to the preservation of the wonderful natural amenities in the area, will make Benfleet a beautiful residential area and an invigorating holiday resort.*

The prediction of growth proved correct and it has continued, spurred on by the expansion of the seaside resort of Southend-on-Sea, the close proximity of London and the far-reaching effects of the

Hadleigh Castle. (Photograph by Ken Porter 2013)

Second World War, which resulted in unprecedented growth in the south-east of Essex. In consequence, the year 1974 saw the merger of the Benfleet Urban District and Canvey Island Urban District Councils, forming the Castle Point Urban District Council, and then in 1992 the authority received borough status.

The names given to the various hundreds in Saxon times were normally derived from the central local meeting place, and later on administrative areas usually retained the same names or adopted similar ones. However, Castle Point broke with tradition by deriving its name from two major landmarks, Hadleigh Castle and Canvey Point.

But where did the names of the original parishes come from?

Benfleet: In Old English '*beam*' means wood and '*fleote*' is the term for stretch of water. Over time, the spelling has varied from Beamfleote, to Beamflet and Benfleota etc., but it seems to have been standardised by the coming of the railway to Benfleet in 1855. There is another small rural area called North Benfleet, but this is part of the Borough of Basildon.

Canvey Island: Although it is commonly believed that the name of Canvey Island is derived from an old Saxon tribe, as the 'Island of Cana's people', in fact the Romans used it. An early map-maker, Claudius Ptolemaeus Ptolemy (90–168AD), a geographer of Alexandria, also showed the area as a series of islands and named it 'Cnossos'.

Hadleigh: Derives its name from the Old English word for village '*haedlege*', which also means 'a heath clearing'. The earliest known reference to Hadleigh dates back to around 1,000AD, although the village does not appear in the Domesday Book, where presumably its lands and livestock were included under Benfleet.

Canvey Point. (Photograph by Ken Porter 2013)

Thundersley: Thundersley is derived from the name of the Anglo-Saxon God of Thunder, *Thunor*, and the word *ley* is Old English for wood/clearing, meaning 'Thunor's wood or clearing'. This part of Essex does not possess many ancient buildings to display its history. Apart from the ruins of Hadleigh Castle and some very old churches, there is little else aside from the Thames Estuary and all its hidden history. Over the centuries, Essex has been described as flat and dull, yet this is what Reginald A. Beckett had to say in his 1901 book, published just 13 years before the outbreak of the Great War:

> *The general ignorance of Essex is still astonishing. Here is a beautiful district lying at our very doors, which to the majority of travellers from the metropolis, is a veritable unknown land. Yet the historic interest, at least, of a county situated so near to London and the Thames and necessarily the theatre of many events that have helped to shape our destinies, must be obvious enough.*

The Castle Point district is a mixture of high ground, low marsh areas and creeks running down to the River Thames, which has historically allowed many different peoples to step ashore. The first recorded inhabitants of the area were the Celtic Trinovantes, with the Romans arriving next, then the Anglo Saxons. The Vikings later took hold of the area, before being defeated at the Battle of Benfleet in 894AD by the army of King Alfred, under the command of his son, Edward the Elder, and son-in-law, Earl Æthelred of Mercia. Subsequently, a church was built by the Saxons in thanksgiving for the victory, on the site now occupied by St Mary's Church.

In 1215 King John gave the village of Hadleigh to Hubert de Burgh, who built the castle and acted as the trustee of the two important castles in southern England, Windsor and Dover. Hubert was a trusted follower of the King and during Henry III's minority he became the effective ruler of England. Unfortunately, he later fell out with the young King and all his lands were confiscated, including Hadleigh. Although the castle stayed in the hands of the monarch, it was not until the reign of Edward II a century later that it began to be used as a royal residence. Edward II's son, Edward III, spotted the strategic importance of the castle as an ideal base for defending the Thames Estuary against the

French. He extended the castle and also built Queenborough Castle on the opposite Kent shore. It later became Edward III's favourite retreat but his successors took little interest in it, and when the castle was eventually sold to Lord Riche in 1551, he sold it off for building materials.

In the 1600s the Dutch were invited to help reclaim the land around Canvey Island. At first they had to build a barrier to keep the tide out, then they drained the island. The barrier wall they erected survived, in the main, into the mid-twentieth century. Even the dramatic floods of 1953 did not entirely break the wall. The sea water went over the top instead, which resulted in sections at the back of the wall being washed away, causing breaches.

The railway first came to South Benfleet in 1855, via a Tilbury Link to London. Surprisingly, it did not have much immediate impact on the local population, which in 1851 was 1,474. A decade later, six years after South Benfleet Station opened, that figure had only risen by eighty-seven. In 1888 a more direct rail route via Barking came into existence and this, combined with the agricultural depression of the 1880s, had caused a considerable increase in population by 1901, to approximately 3,500. Three years before the outbreak of the First World War another 1,500 people were living in the area.

The Great War had a profound impact not only on the history of Great Britain but also on the whole world. The war remains in our memories as an example of a mismatch between political aims and the price paid by ordinary people. Although the last human witnesses are no longer with us, the First World War remains etched in the collective memory of our nation. No other event in our history has had such a dramatic impact on our national identity. The courage displayed by men and women from all the countries involved has had a lasting effect on attitudes, as well as world geography and politics. It has brought about social change, confirming the importance of international cooperation, partnership and solidarity.

The following chapters consist of the wartime stories of those who lived in the old Castle Point area during the conflict and who, through their courage and self-sacrifice, tried to bring peace to the world. At the end of the war they believed that they had brought about a lasting peace but, as we now know, the terms of this peace merely became the catalyst for another devastating war twenty years later.

CHAPTER 1

The South-East Essex Parishes Before the First World War

It is very difficult now to try and envisage what life was like for our forefathers over a hundred years ago. The railway may have been around for fifty years, but the motor car had only just appeared on the scene. Social change was occurring, yet change happened far more slowly than today.

Most working people were still toiling at least six days a week, although the Bank Acts were giving many the opportunity of a few longer weekends. Education was improving, following the 1870 Education Act, and many new schools were being built. Each of our four south-east Essex parishes now had free, government-established schools, though the children were often called away to help in the fields at harvest time. The Church was also still playing a very prominent part in most local people's everyday lives.

This chapter provides a brief outline of what was going on in the various parishes prior to the war, starting with Canvey Island.

Canvey Island
Canvey Island is a marshy island situated in the estuary of the River Thames. Until 1931 Canvey Island was linked to South Benfleet at low tide by a causeway across the Hadleigh Bay, which was passable via

The crossing from South Benfleet to Canvey Island by ferry. (Postcard)

stepping stones or by horse and cart. At high tide, a ferry would transport people across. The island is 6 miles long and 3 miles wide. It is a very rich grazing ground and has a large quantity of arable land. A local coastguard station was manned by a station master and six men. The Chapman Lighthouse, built in 1851, stood half a mile off the island, due south-east, until 1957 when it was demolished; a bell buoy marks the spot today.

In his 1901 book *Romantic Essex*, R.A. Beckett refers to the description of the island by Robert Buchan in his novel *Andromeda* (1900):

Crossing from South Benfleet to Canvey Island on stepping stones. (Postcard)

Left-hand side of the Lobster Smack. (Postcard, pre-1914)

Flat as a map, so intermingled with creeks and runlets that it is difficult to say where water ends and land begins, Canvey Island lies, a shapeless octopus, right under the high ground of Benfleet and Hadleigh and stretches out muddy and slimy feelers to touch and dabble in the deep water of the flowing Thames.

In the opening paragraph Buchan also notes: 'There stood in the loneliest part of Canvey Island, at the mouth of the Thames, a solitary tumbledown inn, called the Lobster Smack. – From time to time the little inn resounded with the merriment of such wayfarers but as a rule it was as deserted as its surroundings.'

Right-hand side of the Lobster Smack. (Photograph by Ken Porter, 2014)

Buchan gives a fictitious name for the landlord of the Lobster Inn, but the real landlord as far back as 1881 was Charles Beckwith, who ran the establishment with the help of his family. By 1911 his son had taken over the management, and the inn had remained in the family for at least thirty years.

Essex farmers were particularly hit hard following the agricultural depression of the 1880s and many sold plots to land speculators. In 1899 Frederick Hester purchased Leigh Beck Farm and laid out 1,004 plots to develop the Southview Estate, which consisted of two-room bungalows erected on concrete footings. His aim was to create a holiday resort and alongside the estate he built a Winter Garden, which was to be followed by a pier, pavilion, boating lake, marine arcade and a mono-rail. Unfortunately, his ideas were too ambitious and the land sales did not keep up with the expenditure, so within five years the administrators moved in.

The population of Canvey Island in 1901 was 307, which had increased to 583 a decade later. Seventy per cent of the male working population in 1901 was employed on the surrounding farms; by 1911 this had dropped dramatically to 40 per cent. The next biggest form of employment among local men was working on the construction of the

Canvey Coast Guard Station. (Postcard)

Kynoch Hotel on Canvey Island. (Postcard pre-1915)

sea wall, which occupied eleven men in 1901 and six in 1911. The local coastguard followed with six staff. Perhaps the most interesting occupation listed in 1901 was that of the winkle fisher.

By 1911, with the increase in visitors to the island and the decline in farming, other types of employment appeared in the census, with shopkeepers and assistants, carpenters, builders, secretaries and solicitors clerks, gardeners, and factory workers. Another change was a boost in female employment. Very few local women were noted as engaging in paid work in the 1901 census and most were either in service, teaching or employed by the inns as bar maids. By 1911, however, there was a much greater number at work, with 41 per cent still in service, but others employed within a variety of new roles – in dress-making, as shop assistants, and at the Hotel Kynoch.

The Hotel Kynoch was built in 1900, taking its name from the Kynoch Explosive Factory, near Stanford le Hope. It was initially intended to accommodate the factory directors and their associates. In 1907 a long jetty was built at the front of the hotel, linking up with the sea wall, yet, like most areas of Canvey in those days, it was fairly isolated.

The memories of a local man, B. Flight (published in the *Essex Countryside* magazine, August 1965), help to paint a picture of what Canvey Island was like on the cusp of the First World War:

I suppose my parents must have been among the first visitors to Canvey Island fifty-five years ago (1910) when they purchased some land for camping. The plot of land they purchased cost one pound per plot. Our early tents were pitched in a large open meadow, flat as all land on the island, with no other habitation between us and the distant sea wall wending its way round the island's circumference.

In those days the island was virtually an immense enclosed meadow, green and peaceful. On a summer day, with larks singing above against the low buzz of grasshoppers, or in the cool evening with the plaintive call of curlews coming from the saltings, one had a sense of repose and contentment rarely found these days.

Flight goes on to explain that their bell tent eventually gave way to a small bungalow, then a larger one and eventually the bell tent only came out if they had a large party. Travelling to and from the island was a bit of a novelty, as it involved either a trip by ferry (usually a rowing boat) or a walk across the stepping stones at low tide. A horse-drawn trap would be available for those who had hired one a few days beforehand, but tourists still had to struggle with their luggage across the fields.

Visitors often walked along the sea wall to the Lobster Smack, which was one of the most romantic old inns you could hope to come across. According to legend, it was once a smugglers' inn, an impression strengthened by the fact that the coastguard station was situated directly opposite. After reading this description, one can understand why Canvey Island was slowly becoming a holiday resort, especially for trippers from East London. One of the first indications that Canvey could be a seaside holiday resort comes from Charles Dickens Jr's publication *Dictionary of the Thames (from Oxford to the Nore)* of 1880: 'There is a fine shell bay and beach, which nearly at all times of the tide is a most pleasant walk close to the sea.'

South Benfleet
Now, after taking a short walk or horse and cart across the causeway, we arrive in South Benfleet on the mainland. The next port of call is the railway station, which opened in 1855, with the line running from

Southend via Tilbury to Barking and Fenchurch Street Station in London.

Of the four parishes within the Castle Point area, in the Edwardian period Benfleet was the only one with a railway station. As previously mentioned, initially the railway had little impact on the 1851 population of 570, which rose by just sixteen in twenty years. In 1888, when the direct rail link via Upminster, Barking and London came into being, the 1891 census reveals that the population fell to 575. Though it had doubled by 1901, this was no doubt due to the agricultural depression and the fact that it had become more affordable to travel into London by rail for employment. South Benfleet was becoming part of the commuter belt.

There was, however, at least one unhappy local commuter, who did not like the noisy, uncomfortable wooden seats, which lacked cushions:

Then hip hurrah for the Tilbury Line
That to 'read-less' lights and dirt incline;
And hurrah for the streams of filth that flow
By the banks of fair Upton and pretty Plaistow!

And hip hurrah for the winds that rill
Through the open 'thirds' with deadly chill;
And hurrah for the jars and the jolts and the shakes -
For the bobbing springs and the back that aches!

Hurrah for the dead cats and kettles and pots
That adorn the banks in picturesque lots,
Where odoriferous breezes play
O'er the happy traveller on his way.

I dreamt last night on my dark home ride
I took staff and directors with mighty stride,
Beneath a moon darkened with mighty stride,
And smothered the lot in Southend mud!

(Author unknown.)

Returning to the station, on the right, round a sharp right-hand bend, there is a stiff hill to climb. It leads into the village of South Benfleet

The Hoy and Helmet Inn. (Photograph by Ken Porter, 2013)

and, ignoring the modern traffic, it is easy to imagine what a pretty little village it was a century ago, with its pubs, blacksmith's forge, village shop and church.

The Hoy and Helmet Inn, built around the early sixteenth century, is the first building you come to in South Benfleet, just up from the bend on the left. The Benfleet Creek came more or less up to the inn, where hay bales would be loaded for transportation to London to feed cab-horses and the animals' manure would be brought back on the return trip for the farms. Next to the Hoy and Helmet was the local blacksmith's forge, which would occasionally be reached by flood water when the creek overflowed. In 1914 the local blacksmith was a woman, Mrs Emma Clark, although she may have been the proprietor of the business, hiring employees to carry out the physical labour at the forge. Harry Thorogood, who took over the business in the late 1920s, went out to France in the First World War to shoe horses.

On the opposite side of the road is the eighteenth century Crown Inn, now known as the Half Crown Pub, and further up the hill, just past the Hoy and Helmet is the village church, St Mary's, built over 1,000 years ago. Then a left turn at a road junction heads in a northerly direction, towards today's major Southend to London Road, the A13.

The Half Crown Inn. (Photograph by Ken Porter, 2013)

Returning to the junction on the opposite corner to the church is the Anchor Inn, which is believed to have been built 600 years ago.

Towards the top of the hill, the Benfleet Downs tumble towards the creek and the Thames, with its sailing ships and barges, and Canvey Island, with its golden cornfields and sheep. Harry Richardson's 1969 reminiscences reveal that the creek used to be full of flat fish, cockles could be raked up and there were winkle beds on the South Benfleet

The Anchor Inn. (Photograph by Ken Porter, 2013)

side of the creek, perhaps plundered by the winkle fisherman living on Canvey Island. In addition, there were plenty of eels and clams which local fishermen used to sell in the pubs, five for a penny, or send them up to London.

The fishermen used to put their nets across the creek at full tide to catch the fish, and they would also put lines of hooks out, but more often than not the crabs escaped with the bait. Although there was much farming going on locally, South Benfleet was also known as a fishing village. In addition, there were two brick fields in the area and, according to Harry Richardson, barges came up to the wharf landing to unload cement and cinder ashes for the brickfields, reloading with the finished bricks.

The Rev A.C Holthouse, who came to the parish in 1914, wrote a letter to the parish magazine about the village: 'South Benfleet may not be what is called an ideal village but it is certainly a pretty one. The abundance of beautiful red-tiled houses showing among the green trees, the glimpse of the river … these are the things which strike one coming here for the first time.'

Kelly's Directory for 1914 notes that the population had increased by 300 to 1,305 by 1911. It also gives an indication of the types of shops in the area, which included: a butcher, dairy, grocers, greengrocers, newsagent, Post Office, boot-maker, hairdresser, coal merchant, baker, hardware shop, refreshment room and even a taxidermist.

Farming was no longer the main occupation for local working men, as a large amount of farm land had been sold off for building, due to the late nineteenth century agricultural depression. Instead, a plot-land environment was slowly being established. Following the agricultural depression of the 1880s many farmers went bankrupt and their farms were sold to land speculators who, in turn, sold off the land into small plots for individual housing developments.

Hadleigh

Continuing along the Benfleet Downs Road for a few miles, you will eventually come across the village of Hadleigh, which is not only famous for its castle but also for its Salvation Army Farm colony. The colony was established by William Booth in 1891, when he purchased Castle Park Farm, Sayers Farm and Park Farm, along with

General William Booth. (Postcard, dated 1908)

approximatively 900 acres of farm land. It was an ideal spot for Booth's vision of a farm colony for the destitute, not too far from London.

The only drawback was that the farm land around Hadleigh was poor, in fact locally it was known as the 'Hadleigh badlands'. Nevertheless, this did not hamper the Salvation Army's ambitions and work progressed rapidly. By the late 1890s three more farms had been purchased: Leigh Park, Leigh Heath and Leigh Marsh Farm. The Army now owned over 3,000 acres, part of which was situated in the neighbouring parish of Leigh-on-Sea.

The locals were initially very sceptical towards the colony and many were openly hostile to the idea of having their small community clustered around its Norman Church, invaded by people they saw as

Dormitories at the Salvation Army Colony, Hadleigh. (Postcard)

Salvation Army, Pig Farm. (Photograph by Ken Porter, 2013)

'down and outs' from East London. The following report published in the *Essex Newsman* on 26 September 1891, highlights the locals' initial concerns:

A LIVELY SCENE IN GENERAL BOOTH'S COLONY NEAR SOUTHEND

Since the first batch of men arrived at the Salvation Army Social Wing farm colony at Hadleigh about forty men have either left or been expelled. Half of these were dismissed for idleness and drinking, for there is a drink shop within a mile of the colony. The other half left of their own accord, being dissatisfied with the work or the food. There has been, with one exception, apparent harmony between the colonists and the officers of the army.

About a month ago four men were dismissed for drunkenness, profanity and disobedience. One of these was a discharged soldier and had been dismissed from the colony on a previous occasion but had been reinstated on a promise of amendment. These four men returned and caused a disturbance, which was perplexing at first, as there was but one policeman in the district and he was more than a mile distant and the intruders swore that they had come to fight and meant to do it. Among the officers at the colony there is a muscular man of slight build who has had 25 years experience in India in the army as a horse-breaker. He belonged to the class known as rough-riders. Like David before Goliath, the little officer stood forth to fight and like David conquered his opponent.

When he related the adventure to me (writes a correspondent of the Manchester Guardian) he said: 'We did all we could to save that discharged, but it warn't no use. We were obliged to turn him out at last. He grumbled at his victuals at dinner and he grumbled at his tea and he would do no work if he could help it. We fed him, we clothed him, we loved him, we prayed for him but we couldn't let the army be trampled on. So I just set to and gave him a licking and made his heels fly up in the air. I did it twice and

Salvation Army postcard, pre-1920.

I did it a third time, until he knew what a rough rider was made of and then he was satisfied.' 'And did you ever speak to the general himself?' I inquired. 'Yes! Yes!' he replied; 'he's had his arms around my neck.'

There is little more to be said at present concerning the colony. It is an experiment and is to be carried on for some time experimentally – that is to say, all questions as to the permanence of the colonists on the estate or their speedy removal to colonies abroad will be decided by actual test of the practicability of both schemes. For the present it is enough to say that all the officers are delighted to find that a far larger proportion of the unemployed are willing to remain and to work than they expected at the outset.

As it turned out, the locals had little to fear, as any problems arising in the colony were controlled within the confines of the site. Many local people also found employment at the colony, especially in the three brick-fields later established there. The experiment turned out to be a success in many ways and it is still going strong today as an employment training centre, a function reminiscent of its origins.

The introduction of a farm colony to the area is one of the reasons for the greater increase in population in Hadleigh compared to the other parishes over this period. The population of the village in 1891 was 526, yet by 1901 it had risen to 1,343 and over the next decade increased even further, to 1,707. Hadleigh was also situated on the main thoroughfare for holiday-makers travelling to the seaside resort of Southend, so although the population around the village was relatively small it was quite a busy community and trade was brisk. Like Benfleet, it had three inns, including The Castle which was built in 1651 and later joined by the Crown and the Wagon and Horses inns during the 1840s.

By 1910 the appearance of mechanical transport alongside the horses and carts caused the junction near the church to be referred to as 'Death Trap Corner', due to the number of accidents and near misses. Locals began calling for a bypass, but it would take another ten years before a speed limit was imposed, and a new road bypassing the church on the other side would not be constructed until 1924.

The Castle Inn. (Photograph by Ken Porter, 2013)

With all the local and passing trade, it is not surprising that by the outbreak of war there were already a number of trades in Hadleigh which would be familiar to inhabitants of the modern village. The 1914 edition of *Kelly's Directory*, lists many of these tradespeople:

Butcher – J. Webster
Greengrocer – Henry Grimes
Grocer – Schofield and Martin
Draper and Post Office – Miss M. Matthews
Chemist – Philip Perkins
General Stores – C. Porter
Confectionery – Miss A. Choppen
Blacksmith – S. Stibbards
Hairdresser – H. Emery [Henry Emery was only seventeen when he started his hairdressing business in 1912, and he ran it until he emigrated to Australia during the Second World War.]

There were many more local tradespeople in the village, including a baker, coal man, dairy man, chimney sweep and a good old English tea room. By 1912 there were forty-one retail shops and many other specialist services being provided in the various cottages scattered around the village. Capital and Counties opened their first bank in Hadleigh in 1910.

By 1914 Hadleigh, with its growing population, was no longer a village but a small town, although many of its inhabitants were still living in primitive conditions, with no gas, nor electricity, running water, or flushing toilets, and most of the roads were still rough tracks. These were problems that the other parishes were also suffering from, and most would not be overcome until well into the 1920s and 1930s.

Thundersley

North of Hadleigh and South Benfleet, is the neighbouring parish of Thundersley. Unlike the other three parishes, Thundersley does not have a waterfront. It also differs slightly in that prior to the First World War the centres of population were based around three separate areas. One centre was situated around St Peter's Church, more or less in the middle of the parish, while the other two lay to the east, at the crossroads by the Woodsman Inn, on the road linking Hadleigh to Rayleigh, and further east lay the Daws Heath area.

St Peter's Church, Thundersley. (Photograph by Ken Porter, 2013)

Daws Heath, Thundersley during the 1800s was renown as a lawless place – not necessarily somewhere you might expect a new religious sect to open up a mission church. Perhaps the founder, James Banyard, saw it as a challenge. In the early 1800s Banyard became a Wesleyan Methodist preacher. He later fell out with the Wesleyans over his preaching, which included divine healing, because he was against doctors being allowed to attend members of the congregations and their children. Banyard broke away from the Wesleyans and founded his own sect. Their first chapel was built in Rochford, Essex in 1850 and they took the name 'The Peculiar People' from a text in Deuteronomy (Chapter 14, verse 2), which states, 'and the Lord hath chosen thee to be a peculiar people unto himself.' It is understood the former lawlessness of the Daws Heath area started to improve dramatically once the Peculiar People moved in, with a number of local ruffians joining the sect.

Another chapel was built at Daws Heath in 1852 and, because of

Peculiar People's Chapel, Daws Heath – now a private residence. (Photograph by Ken Porter, 2014)

growing congregation numbers, a further brick chapel was also required, being built in 1882. This building was demolished in 1976 when a new chapel was put up, yet it is now a private residence. The name 'Peculiar People' was discontinued in 1956, replaced by 'The Union of Evangelical Churches'.

The 1914 edition of *Kelly's Directory* notes that the parish of Thundersley consisted of approximatively 2,545 acres, and that other nearby areas covered by the small hamlets were principally made up of pasture and small holdings. The population in 1911 stood at 1,434, and though lower than neighbouring Hadleigh it had in fact seen a greater increase over the previous decade. This was probably due, not just to the agricultural depression and the railways, but also to the fact that the southern and northern boundaries of the parish had two major link roads to London and Southend on Sea, (the northern boundary road is now the A127 and the southern road is the A13).

Changing Times

In the early 1900s, throughout Britain welfare reforms were taking place. The Liberal Party had come to power in 1906 on the back of proposed welfare reforms. One of the first reforms they carried out was the Old-Age Pensions Act in 1908, which was implemented in January 1909 for those over the age of seventy.

However, the criteria that applicants had to meet to obtain the new State pension of 5 shillings a week (worth around £23 in 2013) or 7 shillings and 6 pence (worth around £34 in 2013) for a married couple was very harsh. Applicants also had to pass a character test, have worked all their lives and possess an income of less than £21 10 pence per year. The benefit was set deliberately low to encourage workers to make their own provision for retirement, and only half a million people were eligible for it of the population of 46 million.

In 1911 another landmark piece of welfare legislation, the first National Insurance Act, was passed and came into effect in July 1912. The idea behind it was to create a national insurance system for working people, to protect them against illness and unemployment. It covered wage earners between the ages of sixteen and seventy, who had to contribute 4 pence per week, in addition to 3 pence from their employers and 2 pence from the state. In return workers were entitled to a level of free medical care and 7 shillings per week unemployment

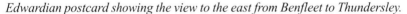

Edwardian postcard showing the view to the east from Benfleet to Thundersley.

benefit for up to fifteen weeks per year. At that time there was very little free medical care, other than within the workhouse, and relatively few doctors willing to provide low-cost care. One doctor often covered several parishes, and this was certainly the case in the four parishes discussed in this book.

Another major difference between modern and Edwardian society is that before the First World War only about 20 per cent of families owned their own property, whereas in some areas today, around 70 per cent own their homes. However, in the south-east of Essex this situation was changing, possibly even faster than elsewhere, because plots of land were becoming available for development, enabling many families to buy a plot and erect a small building to live in. Planning regulation and permission was still very haphazard, so they had little red tape to deal with.

In pre-war Britain minor legislative changes to the welfare system were making big differences to the lives of ordinary people throughout the country. Meanwhile, our four south-east Essex parishes were seeing greater growth in the first fourteen years of the twentieth century than in the previous century, due to the arrival of the railway, land becoming available for development and the expansion of the nearby seaside resort of Southend. Despite all this growth, for many, living standards were still very primitive. When, in August 1914, Sir Edward Grey commented in Parliament, 'The lights have gone out all over Europe', Benfleet and the other parishes had never been lit up and would not have electricity until well into the 1920s.

However, as Britain faced involvement in a worldwide conflict, parochial problems of water supply, sewage, road conditions and rubbish collections would have to be put on hold.

CHAPTER 2

Footsteps to War

Why did Britain have to go to war in 1914? Throughout history Great Britain has become involved in various international conflicts, but on this occasion the British Government did not want to go to war. To understand what happened in 1914, we need to go back in time and trace events in Europe following the final defeat of the French at the Battle of Waterloo in 1815. After this point, Britain tended to keep out of European affairs and concentrated instead on cementing ties with its Empire, aside from the Crimean War of 1853–1856 .

The Crimean War was initially a religious war, however, and it appears that Britain became involved due to concerns about Russian aggression against the Ottoman (Turkish) Empire. Britain posited itself as standing up for the underdog. *Punch* portrayed this sentiment in an 1854 cartoon showing Britannia wielding the Sword of Justice, with a lion at her side, ready to rescue the weak against tyrants and bullies. Many of the same emotive forces were at work when Britain decided to go to war against the Germans in 1914, this time in defence of 'Little Belgium'.

Shortly after the turbulent Napoleonic era, in 1817 Serbia gained independence from the Ottoman Empire, becoming a principality within the growing Austrian Empire, followed by the Greeks in 1829. In 1830 the United Kingdom of Netherlands split and Belgium and Luxembourg gained independence, although Luxembourg lost half of its territory. The Italian War of Independence ended in 1860 with the unification of Italy.

The the Prussian victory in the Austro-Prussian War resulted in the formation of the Austria-Hungarian Empire in 1867. France then became concerned about the emerging power of Prussia and the unification of the various German states. Prussia, on the other hand, realised that unification between Prussia and the Northern and Southern German states would not happen unless there was a war against France. When a Prussian Prince became a candidate for the throne of Spain, France, fearing encirclement by an allied Prussia and Spain, declared war on 19 July 1870. After a series of swift Prussian and German victories, the German states proclaimed their union and Germany became a nation-state. The Treaty of Frankfurt of 1871 gave Germany most of Alsace and parts of Lorraine, and this territory became a major factor in France's involvement in the First World War.

There was then a short period of peace before tensions in the Balkans exploded. The turmoil started with the Russian victory in their 1878 war with Turkey, which led to considerable changes within the Balkan region of Europe, with many Balkan nations gaining independence. This was the real beginning of the fall of the Ottoman Empire. At this time Austria also gained Bosnia and Herzegovina from the Ottoman Empire, a measure that was complicated by the fact that most Bosnians were Muslim and preferred to stay within the Ottoman Empire.

Since the Crimean War, apart from exerting a little pressure here and there, and seizing control of the Suez Canal in 1888, Britain had kept aloof from the problems in Europe and the Balkans. The British Government was more concerned with a number of smaller conflicts throughout the British Empire, such as the Zulu War of 1879, the Boer Wars of 1880 and 1899–1901. During this period many other smaller conflicts were going on around the world, including the 1899–1901 Boxer Rebellion in China. The Chinese took on an eight-nation alliance, involving: Britain, Russia, Germany, Austria-Hungary, Italy, France, Japan and the United States. Many of these countries would fight against each other a decade later. The Rebellion was put down and China was forced to pay heavily for the defeat.

Other internal conflicts were also occurring during the early years of the twentieth century: Russia lost a war to Japan in 1905, resulting in the Russian Revolution of the same year; Norway gained independence from Sweden in 1905; and in 1912 Italy took Libya away from the Ottoman Empire. All these intrigues, conflicts and machinations increased distrust amongst the European nations, who all appeared to be engaged in power games that could only end in war.

In October 1912, Bulgaria, Greece, Montenegro and Serbia (all previously part of the Ottoman Empire) formed the Balkan League and attacked the Ottoman Empire. As a result, the Ottoman Empire lost virtually all its remaining Balkan territory. Then, on 16 June 1913, dissatisfied with the division of spoils, Bulgaria attacked Serbia and Greece in a second, much shorter Balkan conflict.

There is no doubt that these wars and the the preceding century of conflicts set the scene for the First World War. Austria-Hungary was concerned by the growing strength of Serbia, now allied with its former enemy Russia; the Ottoman Empire and Bulgaria were happy to fall in with Austria-Hungary and the growing strength of Germany, in the hope of recovering lost territory.

On the other hand, Britain was becoming increasingly wary of German aggression, which was then fostering distrust among the various European powers. Kaiser Wilhelm II had set Germany on a course to compete with Britain to become the world's most dominant super-power, by expanding the German overseas empire and also gaining territory in the east, at the expense of Russia.

Britain and Germany (formerly Prussia) had been allies since the days of Napoleon. However, following the Crimean War, the aggressive German approach had pushed Britain into a closer alliance with France and Russia against Germany.

All of this boils down to four main reasons for the outbreak of war in 1914:

- **Nationalism** – National pride was flourishing among the various countries and states of Europe and many ethnic groups craved independent nation status.
- **Imperialism** – The major European countries held many overseas colonies and new lands were being contested by them.
- **Militarism** – As nationalism and imperialism took hold, so greater military strength to defend their possessions appeared increasingly necessary to the European powers.
- **Lack of International Organisation** – There was no international governing body to help solve the various conflicts, such as NATO or the United Nations until after the Second World War.

By 1914 the political situation in Europe was very tense indeed and all the situation needed was a spark to ignite world war, which soon arrived. Some Bosnia Serbs had been angered by the annexation of Bosnia by Austria and a visit to Sarajevo by the heir to the throne of Austria-Hungary Archduke, Franz Ferdinand, and his wife gave them an opportunity to demonstrate their fury. Their political objective was to break off Austria-Hungary's south Slav provinces and establish a Greater Serbia.

On 28 June 1914, six young assassins trained by Serbian Military Intelligence waited for the Archduke's car, as it drove along the main road towards Sarajevo. The first conspirator threw a bomb at the car but missed and was arrested. The Archduke decided to cancel the visit and return home by a different route. Unfortunately, nobody had told the driver of the change and when he realised he stopped the car to turn it around. The car halted in front of Gavrilo Princip, one of the conspirators, who was on his way home, believing the group had failed. He immediately pulled out his pistol and shot Franz Ferdinand, then in the following tussle he also shot the Archduke's wife Sophie.

A chain reaction followed, with Austria-Hungary initially demanding that Serbia investigate the assassination and implement harsh punishment against the suspected assassins. Serbia was on the verge of complying, but then Russia offered support. This resulted in Austria declaring war on Serbia on 28 July 1914 and invading the country on 12 August. The third Balkan war had started, which subsequently became the Great War and later the First World War.

Though Russia was unprepared for war, it chose to support its smaller neighbour. The Russian Foreign Minister summoned the Austrian ambassador, declaring, 'This means a European War, you are setting Europe alight.' The Russians immediately called upon France to comply with the terms of the Triple Entente signed by Russia, France and Britain in 1904.

The next question was how would Britain respond? The remoteness of the Balkan theatre and the fact that neither Russia or France had been threatened made it difficult to persuade the British cabinet and the public that intervention was necessary. However, Germany then declared war against France on 1 August 1914, deciding to attack France through Belgium. Britain had signed a treaty with Belgium back in the 1830s and was committed to aid France and Belgium in the event of war. Therefore, the British Government had no alternative but to declare war on Germany, at 21.00pm on 4 August, after the British ultimatum requesting German troops to leave Belgium soil was ignored. This was followed by an announcement to the nation at 23.17pm, that 'a state of war exists between Great Britain and Germany.'

The first British troops arrived in France on 8 August. The war to end all wars had begun, but was Britain, or indeed were any of the other nations involved, ready for such a war? Although Britain still had the largest navy in the world, its professional army was a very tiny contingent compared with the vast conscript armies of France, Russia and Germany. However, according to one British historian, Brigadier James Edwards Edmonds, writing in 1925, the British Army in 1914 was the best equipped, trained and organised that the country had ever sent to war.

Unlike the French, whose soldiers wore highly visible blue coats and red trousers in the early months of the war, the British wore a form of camouflage uniform first adopted in the Indian and Colonial wars. Improved during the Second Boer War, by 1902 British Army uniform consisted of dark khaki serge. Its weakness was the peaked cloth cap, which gave very little protection and this is now seen as one of the reasons why so many men were killed in the early months of the war. Fortunately, in 1915 the Brodie Helmet or 'Tommy's Helmet' made out of heavy steel was designed. Initially there were insufficient Brodie Helmets to go around, so they were only issued to those on the Front Line. It was not until the spring of 1916 that large quantities of the helmets finally became available for all military personnel.

Although Germany was concerned about Britain joining the conflict, perhaps due to the recent Balkan wars they were convinced that many colonies under British rule would take advantage of the war to rebel, thereby reducing Britain's war effort. This turned out to be a huge miscalculation, as citizens of the British Empire flocked to help the 'mother country'. Recruits from Canada, Australia and New Zealand came first, followed by South Africa and India – they came from all parts of the Empire. The Colonies not only sent troops but also food supplies, such as tinned salmon, bags of flour, cheese and even horses, which the British armed forces were in desperate need of. Horses were to play a considerable part in the war effort, not necessary

First World War propaganda: a recruitment postcard.

within the cavalry but in moving supplies and equipment around at the Front.

The British Expeditionary Force (BEF) comprised initially of less than 200,000 men, immediately saw action at Mons, in Belgium, near the French border, where they put up a gallant defence at Le Cateau. The Allies were, however, forced to retreat in the face of a German onslaught. The retreat continued until the middle of September, when the Allies managed to stop the Germans at the River Marne, where the British had moved into position to protect the Channel ports and keep their supplies and communication routes open.

The invasion of Belgium en route to invading France was all part of Germany's Schlieffen Plan, devised in December 1905 by General Count Alfred Von Schlieffen. He believed that any future war was going to be fought initially on the Western Front and that France posed more of a military threat to Germany than Russia. His solution was to attack and defeat France to deter Britain from getting involved, then turn his attention to Russia.

Although, it appeared that Britain had been forced into war for lack of a viable alternative, the declaration of war was met in many cases with enthusiasm and excitement. Yet, in Government there were factions against joining the conflict. Lord Morley, Mr John Burns and

Mr C.P. Trevelyan all resigned from the cabinet and the Neutrality League took a full-page advertisement in the national newspapers on 5 August, which consisted of the following text:

> *ENGLISHMEN, DO YOUR DUTY*
> *And Keep Your Country Out of a*
> *WICKED AND STUPID WAR*

It was too late: men and youths from all walks of life were flocking to join up. Anyway, most people believed that this was going to be the war to end all wars and over by Christmas.

The chief players now emerged. They were made up of the Central Powers – Germany, Austria-Hungary, the Ottoman Empire, Bulgaria, Finland, and Azerbaijan (Lithuania would join later, in 1918, once Russia had dropped out). Just before the war, Italy had been in an alliance with Germany, but refused to participate in the conflict and in fact later joined the Allies. The Allies included: France, Russia, Britain, Serbia and later USA, Romania and Italy. The long list of participants shows what a mess continental Europe had got into.

Map showing the locations of the Central Powers and the Allies. (Drawing by Sue Ranford)

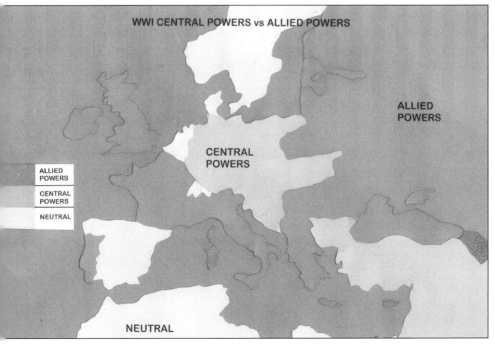

CHAPTER 3

Home Front

While conflict raged across Europe, our four south-east Essex parishes were prospering, Hadleigh in particular. Now the war would put a temporary halt to any real improvements, as life changed overnight. But what was it really like for the families at home, waiting daily for news of loved ones at the Front for four long years? Now we can have instant updates from almost anywhere in the world, but then families often had to wait months to hear from their loved ones or receive confirmation of their fate.

There is no doubt that the declaration of war against Germany was a tremendous shock to the majority of people in Britain. There was widespread disbelief, in spite of newspaper reports warning of a war at hand. This possibility might have been accepted by the public, but few people imagined that Britain would be in it. As there had been so many recent conflicts on the European mainland, it seemed to Britons that this would be just another overseas skirmish.

The British public and Government at the time were more concerned with the growing industrial agitation; the working classes were beginning to take mass industrial action during a period that became known as the 'Great Unrest'. The suffragette movement was also gaining momentum and the problems in Ireland were intensifying. It is possible that the British public had been lulled into a false sense of security and had become more concerned with tumultuous home affairs.

Nevertheless these troubling situations were rapidly overtaken by the developments in Europe. An industrial truce was immediately called by the union leaders and industrial strikes were dramatically reduced. The militant suffragettes of the WSPU agreed to halt all activism in support of the war effort. The implementation of the Irish Home Rule Bill, although placed on the statute book, was suspended until the conflict was over.

These domestic problems were overshadowed by a call to arms, with thousands of enthusiastic men rushing to enlist. Meanwhile, civilians began panic-buying and hoarding food. The situation was so severe in some places, that retailers had to close early and prices rose rapidly. For example on the morning of the declaration of war, 5 August 1914, one pound of sugar was sold at 2 1/2 pence, but by the evening this had risen to 6 pence.

The national papers of the time give the impression that this panic was widespread, but this is not the case in the local papers. Sleepy little villages in the countryside, like our four south-east Essex parishes, were more self-sufficient and far less affected by shortages. Even the poorest families tended to grow their own vegetables and have livestock, at least some chickens. In the country, lack of food was not such an important issue, and certainly not when compared with the loss of men folk and the possibility of alien spies in the area.

Foreign Internees in the First World War
The outbreak of war raised genuine fears amongst the populace of a potential German invasion and there was a considerable amount of initial scaremongering with regards to foreign immigrants. In fact anyone with a foreign name, accent or appearance came under suspicion as a possible spy.

Before the war the Government had already compiled a secret list of 'aliens' (foreign nationals), which revealed that over 28,000 people of foreign extraction were then resident in Britain, including 11,000 of German or Austrian origin. The 1911 census revealed that there were over 5,000 aliens in Essex, including 3,000 Germans and Austrians, of which 1,000 were naturalised British citizens. This was obviously of some concern locally, because of the vast Essex coastline and inland waterways, which would make it fairly easy for foreign aliens to slip in and out of the country without detection.

The day after war broke out, the British Government passed the Alien Restriction Act, whereby aliens had to register with the police, and adhere to regulations restricting their movement. In some cases they were moved away from prohibited areas or into internment camps. Southend had three internment ships moored just off the end of the pier for a time. Scouts were given the task of patrolling road and rail routes, just in case enemy aliens decided to interfere with telegraph lines.

In the cities, the windows of shops owned by German residents were smashed and suspicion was rife. If a neighbour spotted a pigeon landing on your house, you could immediately became a suspect, as happened in Basildon to Henry Ernest Ubele a local German resident. Ubele, a naturalised Briton of 25 years standing, was arrested by the military on suspicion of using carrier pigeons to convey messages to the enemy. He was taken away by five soldiers, various checks were carried out, and his barn and premises were searched, but nothing was found. It turned out that Ubele did not keep pigeons. The case was dropped, although he was threatened with deferred internment.

Everyone was scrutinised and even priests with foreign-sounding names came under suspicion. G.M. Behr, the priest in charge of St Stephen's Colchester, took to the pages of his parish magazine to prove his innocence.

Tourists to south-east Essex were equally at risk. John Kingsley was born in Germany in 1865 and he became a British national in 1901. At some point he had decided to change his birth name to the more Anglicised Jacob Schmitt. Kingsley worked as a confectioner and lived in Clapham Junction, South London, but he frequently visited Leigh Beck, Canvey Island. He was recommended for internment by the police in the event of a national emergency, but as he was not a permanent resident in the area this was not carried out.

Careful checks were made on the inhabitants of local hotels and lodging houses. On 24 November 1914, the General Officer commanding the Thames and Medway Defences, Chatham wrote to the manager of Hotel Kynoch on Canvey Island, asking for enquiry to be made as to the characters of the current occupants. Enquiries were made by the police, who reported the following occupants residing at the hotel on 31 December 1914:

Miss Hall the current Licensee
Douglas Hemmo who is taking over the Licence
Lieutenants Jacobs, Stewart and Houghton, who are

employed on the Admiralty Cutters patrolling the river
Mr, Mrs, and Miss Jacobs, the father, mother and sister of
Lieutenant Jacobs
Mrs Houghton, the mother of Lieutenant Houghton
One domestic and a house boy

The police confirmed that the hotel was the property of Kynochs Ltd, who also owned the adjoining property and there did not appear to be any other suspicious activity.

Not all Britons with German connections were discreet after the outbreak of war; some even deliberately drew attention to themselves. Harry Moulin Rome from Putney, London, and his German-born wife Minna were living on Canvey Island in 1914. In the 1911 census the couple claimed to be retired, although they were then in their early thirties. Harry had apparently made his fortune through the oyster trade and he was considered eccentric, with bad drinking habits, and heavily under the influence of his wife.

Several complaints about his conduct were made to the police and, at the time of the explosion on HMS *Chatham* on 27 May 1915, Harry allegedly laughed in the faces of his neighbours while they were anxiously discussing the matter. People therefore had doubts about his loyalty and, following police investigation, the couple were recommended for expulsion, under the Defence of the Realm Regulations. Harry and Minna left Canvey Island for Marlow, Buckinghamshire in July 1915 and do not appear to have returned to the island after the war, even though the order against them was revoked in January 1919.

Another strange case was that of Nissim Levi, born in Turkey, who had become a naturalised Briton before the war. In 1911 he was living with his wife Lettice and their three daughters and two sons at Pier View Lodge, Canvey Island. The family were wealthy enough to employ three servants and a governess, as Nissim ran a successful business as an oriental carpet importer. Nissim was either a very respected member of the community or the locals had not realised that Turkey was part of the Ottoman Empire and on the side the Central Powers, as he appears not to have suffered any prejudice. The Levi family were still on the island in 1928.

Also in the 1911 census is Carl Oppermann, a German living with his wife Elizabeth and family at Cumberland Lodge, Cumberland Avenue, in South Benfleet. Carl was a 72-year-old retired engineer and he had been living in Britain since at least 1860, when he had married Elizabeth. It is not known whether he was interned during the war, but the Oppermanns had moved out of the area by the time Carl died in June 1916, as his death was registered in Barnet.

Another South Benfleet resident of foreign extraction seems, like Carl Oppermann, to have been above suspicion, as a long-standing naturalised Briton. Marcus Samuel Bergmann was born in Russia, but became a naturalised Briton in 1881. He lived with his wife Myra at 'Sans Sonci' on Thundersley Park Road throughout the First World War. Marcus was a former missionary and he had worked for the London City Mission in the Hoxton area of East London. The Mission's early work centred on the poor and destitute but it soon developed a wide range of charitable work, including establishing ragged schools and ministering to working people. Marcus died at South Benfleet in 1922.

British nationals, as well as foreigners, could be investigated by the authorities if they were accused of nefarious activities. John Henry Bishop Laggett of South Benfleet received a visit from the police on 18 November 1914, when Alfred Moore, a London auctioneer wrote to the police, suggesting that it would be advisable for them to make an inspection of Laggett's house. The property commanded views of the Thames Estuary and it seems that no one was allowed to enter it on any pretext. The house was inspected by the police, but nothing remotely 'detrimental to the nation's cause' could be found. Mr Laggett was a local special constable and it was believed that the letter may have been written out of spite, as his property was then for sale and prospective buyers were being refused admission to the house until a certain date.

Another local, a Mrs Carpenter from South Benfleet, was interviewed by the police on 19 September 1915, following an anonymous letter sent to a secret service agent, which alleged her to be a German spy. She gave the following statement:

> *I think I know what you mean, some days ago a women living in the neighbourhood who is a busybody and always interfering with other peoples business said to me, 'Mrs*

*Carpenter, you are a German, are you'? I jokingly replied,
'Yes, I think I must be a real Prussian'. I thought no more
of it and had no idea that she would say anything about it
or I would not have said it. I had no idea it would cause all
this trouble. Mrs Carpenter was born in Coggeshall and
was currently living in South Benfleet.*

The matter was dropped but it shows how in wartime even an off-hand remark could be misinterpreted.

A Thundersley man, Thomas Hughes, was investigated by the police simply because he owned a car with bright lights, as glowing car headlights had been seen at Hadleigh on the night of 9 May 1915, during an air raid. Thomas Hughes may have been investigated because a German friend of his daughter, Elizabeth Marguerite Matilda Heine, was staying in Woodcroft in July and August 1914. Elizabeth was among hundreds of German tourists in Britain on the outbreak of war. She returned to Germany at the end of her visit. No action was taken against Thomas Hughes, and the police discovered that a couple from Ilford who owned a car with bright headlights, a Mr and Mrs Desket, had also visited Woodcroft on that night.

Attitudes were far more distrustful towards local aliens, however. In the parish of Hadleigh, Isabel Gilliard, a German, was recorded in the 1911 census as living with her husband William Henry and their five children in Park House, Park Farm. The farm had been taken over by the Salvation Army and both Isabel and William were working as Salvation Army officers. Their fate is not known, but they were no longer living there in 1918. Both died within three months of each other in 1933 at Thornton Heath, Surrey.

An altogether more suspicious character named Kern was living at The Grange, in Daws Heath, Hadleigh. On 7 August 1914, the local authorities received information from the Metropolitan Police that he was a German subject who had for sometime been working in the German and Austrian Embassies and he was suspected of being a spy. The local police made enquiries and confirmed that he was in fact an American, born in Baltimore in 1866. However, he had married a German woman and her brother was working and living with him. Kern was a translator and, although his various papers were carefully examined, nothing was found to confirm the rumours that he was a spy.

He decided to comply with the Aliens Restriction Order and on 27 August left for America.

In Thundersley, the 1911 Census reveals Christian Baner, a German, aged 72, and his wife Mary. The couple were no longer in the area by 1918 and their fate is unknown. Alongside the Baners were a number of other foreigners, all recorded as Russians, save Annie Brockman, a Dutch national, who was running a boarding house. They included: Harris Caplan and his wife Annie, who were living on private means; Louis Fedder, a ladies' tailor and his wife Iva; and Nathan Margolis, an ironmonger and his wife Leah. Only Nathan Margolis and his family were still living there in 1918. Had the rest been driven out due to prejudice? Unfortunately, the local papers do not reveal any clues.

The authorities detected a German citizen in the area, Carl Wilhelm Gustave Tode, who was living at 'Sunnyside' in Thundersley when a War Office report, dated 3 July 1915, was passed to the local police. It stated that he was a German, the former master of an oil ship and that he was suspected of giving information to the enemy. Carl Wilhelm had been born in Prussia but, on 28 December 1896, he and his wife had become naturalised Britons. He had worked as the captain of an oil tank steamer until he was discharged on 21 October 1914, owing to the war and he was currently living on his savings, supporting his wife, two sons and two daughters. The Tode family's house stood in a prominent position on the main road, on high ground overlooking the Thames, but nothing had occurred locally to arouse the suspicions of the police. However, Carl Wilhem was recommended for internment, which he appears to have avoided, after it was deferred.

Sidney Langton – A Boer War and WW1 Hero

A Swiss national, Emilie Langton, was living in New Thundersley with her husband Sidney, a poultry dealer, on the outbreak of war. Although Switzerland was neutral, in the initial hysteria she may have been victimised or mistakenly perceived as German. Yet, it is likely that their neighbours' attention would quickly have been drawn to Sidney's impressive status as a Second Boer War veteran and his continued military career during the First World War.

Sidney Langton was born at Creaton, Northamptonshire in 1880. At the age of eighteen he signed up for the Coldstream Guards and it would appear that he had, for a short period, served with the 3rd

Battalion, Leicester Regiment, before buying himself out and re-enlisting with the Guards. He eventually arrived in Gibraltar with the 1st Battalion on 10 March 1898 and during his time there he decided to sign up for an extended service of seven years for a gratuity payment of £2,000.

After a seven-month stay, the battalion sailed to the Cape, South Africa. The Coldstream Guards website notes that by November 1899 both the 1st and 2nd Battalions were encamped near Orange River Stations and played a very distinguished role in the campaign that followed. They first saw action on 23 November 1899, during an attack at Belmont, which was intended to dislodge the Boers on the ridge, south-west of Mount Blanc. This was achieved before they moved on to Modder River, where initially they were kept in reserve but later had to extend the line, lying all day under heavy fire. Their losses from these two offensives were light, however, and the British managed to force the Boers to withdraw from their positions around the Modder River.

There were further skirmishes at Dreifontian, Johannesburg and Diamond Hill. The Diamond Hill battle took place on 11-12 June 1900 and after 14,000 British soldiers squared up against 4,000 Boers, the British managed to force the opposing troops from their hill positions. In his memoirs, the British General Ian Hamilton remarked that the battle was the turning point in the war, as it ensured that the Boers could not recapture Pretoria.

Sidney was back in Britain for six months of leave in June 1901, after which he returned to South Africa until 4 October 1902. He was eventually discharged on 20 January 1910, after twelve years' service. He was never injured but suffered several bouts of illness which required periods of hospitalisation. During all this activity, he managed to meet Emilie and they married on 12 April 1906, in Marylebone, London.

In 1911, Sidney, Emilie and their five-year-old son were living at the 'Oakes' in Overton Road, New Thundersley. By the end of January 1910, Sidney had re-enlisted in the reserves for another four years, before being discharged on 30 January 1914, only seven months before the outbreak of the First World War. Whether inspired by the British retreat at Mons, a call from the army or his own martial spirit, Sidney re-enlisted into the Coldstream Guards at Southend, joining the 2nd

Battalion this time, at Windsor, on 9 November 1915. His re-enlistment was quite possibly due to a call from the Guards, because in the early days of the war they suffered very heavy losses. For example, on 29 October 1914 at Gheluvelt, the 1st Battalion was left with no officers and only eighty men.

However, it was some eleven months before Sidney found himself at the Front and his first taste of action was probably the Battle of Le Transley, (1 October–5 November 1916). It was the final offensive of the 1916 Battle of the Somme and, as in many of the previous offensives, the result was indecisive. Throughout 1917 the 2nd Battalion and the 4th (which Sidney transferred to on 12 March 1917), were involved in many of the battles that followed, right through to the end of war, commencing with the German retreat to the Hindenburg Line and the Battle of Arras (9 April–16 May)

Sidney was back in Britain for a well-earned rest in November 1917 but he was soon back in the field, where, on 18 April 1918, he was promoted to Lance Corporal and had his pay increased to 5 shillings a week. He was granted leave a few days before the Armistice, then was transferred to the 3rd Battalion just before he was demobbed in February 1919, subsequently joining the Z Army Reserve. Awarded the Victory and British War Medals, in addition to his Boer War Campaign medals, Sidney returned to his peaceful life in Thundersley. In 1929 he was still living at the 'Oakes' with his son and a daughter. The fact that the family remained in the area suggests that Emilie was not persecuted during the war, either because people were aware of her Swiss nationality or because they knew her brave husband was at the Front, fighting on their behalf.

The cases detailed above are just a small sample, but they give a flavour of the suspicion and fear that was present in the early years of the war.

A Hadleigh Internee

The *Chelmsford Chronicle* of 13 December 1918 reported: 'Stoker S. Faux, Royal Fleet Reserve, is at home, 1 Percy Villas, Hadleigh, after internment in Holland.' The Netherlands remained neutral during the conflict, yet the Hague Conventions of 1907 dictated that this neutral nation was obliged to disarm and intern every military man who set foot in the country during wartime.

Stanley Faux was born in Plaistow in 1884, to John and Elsie Faux, and by 1891 the family were living in Hadleigh. In 1911 he married Grace Perkins but they were soon parted by the war, as on 17 September 1914 Stanley joined the Royal Fleet Reserve Hawke Battalion. This battalion was part of the Royal Naval Division, which was composed of the 1st, 2nd and 3rd Royal Naval Brigade under the command of Winston Churchill, the First Sea Lord. The battalions mainly consisted of reservists and Royal Navy volunteers who had been conscripted on 2 August 1914, due to the threat of war, and so while in the training camp they were retrained as infantrymen.

They were given the task of helping the Belgian Army to defend the fortified city of Antwerp. The Germans were threatening to surround the Franco-British forces in order to march into northern France and so, to gain time, it was important to defend Antwerp. By 8 October 1914, it was becoming obvious that the city could no longer be defended and the Belgian and British troops decided to retreat. Due to a number of mishaps, Commodore Wilfred Henderson of the 1st Brigade (which consisted of three battalions, including Hawke's Battalion.) had no other option than to lead his troops into the neutral Netherlands, where they were immediately interned in line with international law.

Several internment camps had been established in the Netherlands, but the main camp for the interned English soldiers was at Groningen and it became known as the 'Engelse Kamp' (English Camp). In total the Netherlands during the whole conflict interned 33,105 Belgians; 1,751 British; 1,461 Germans; 8 French; and 4 American servicemen. Later in the war, to try to stop escapes from the internment camps, the Dutch and British Governments came to an agreement to allow internees leave to travel to the centre of Groningen and, at a later stage, under certain conditions they could go to England for a few weeks, giving their word of honour to return. While they were interned, many servicemen were even allowed to find local employment, as long as they were not seen to be taking employment away from the Dutch.

On 16 October 1916 Stanley Faux benefited from these new rules, when he was allowed home for just over two weeks and again, on 22 January 1918, he had nearly four weeks' leave. He was eventually repatriated, on 5 December 1918, and on returning home he was transferred to the 1st Reserve Battalion. Stanley was awarded the 1914

Star, Victory and British War Medals. He then signed up for another eleven years' service from 1921–1932, for which he was also awarded the Royal Navy Long Service and Good Conduct Medals.

Volunteers and Conscription

'Volunteers, Volunteers,' the cry went out, and they came in their droves: men and women of all walks of life and ages – farm labourers, city clerks, factory workers, the unemployed, the aristocracy. Four months into the war, over one million men in Britain had volunteered.

The following untitled poem appeared in the *Southend Standard* three days after its author, Private Sydney Morris Smith, was killed.

> *T'was early in September*
> *I saw it, by the way -*
> *'Your King and Country need you,*
> *Enlist my lad today!'*
> *I thought the matter over -*
> *A soldier I would be*
> *And help old England free.*
>
> *So odd I went to Southend,*
> *A pleasant town close by;*
> *I saw the colour Sergeant;*
> *and told him I would try.*
> *I went before the doctor,*
> *And – well, you know the rest –*
> *He put mow on the scales mate,*
> *And measured round my chest.*
>
> *Ah Well! A year's gone by;*
> *Things are changed with you and me;*
> *But still I'm busy fighting,*
> *Somewhere far across the sea.*
> *So 'Land of Hope and Glory,'*
> *Forever we will sing*
> *May God give England Victory*
> *And save our gracious King.*

(By Private Sydney Morris Smith, deceased 27 September 1915).

The country had been deluged with newspaper reports, literature and even music hall songs, all urging patriotism and a sense of duty. The last major European conflict that Britain had been involved in was the Crimean War of 1853–1856, and the generation of men now about to go to war had been brought up on with images of martial heroism inspired by this war, in 'The Thin Red Line' and the 'Charge of the Light Brigade'. So it is not surprising that there was such enthusiasm to fight against the perceived tyranny of Germany and her allies. In any case, people believed that it was all going to be over by Christmas.

The need for volunteers between the ages of 19 and 41 was urgent, as on the outbreak of war Britain only had a small regular army of around 200,000 men, plus an army reserve of another 200,000 former soldiers and a further 270,000 volunteer militia, known as Territorials. These soldiers were only committed to serving in the United Kingdom and initially only 7 per cent signed up to serve overseas. This changed very quickly; one of the authors' own grandfathers was among the many Territorials who agreed at a later date to serve overseas.

At that time, Britain and its Empire depended on the Royal Navy for security, so hitherto most of the military budget had been used in maintaining the navy and the standing army was relatively small. Most European countries were in a better military position, due to the fact that they had been at war more frequently during the previous hundred years. They tended to have compulsory conscription for all their male citizens from the age of eighteen. They had also developed a sophisticated and well-rehearsed system of military transportation to mobilise their troops and get them to the Front. Germany and France had four million troops ready for mobilisation, Austria-Hungary had three million and Russia six million. A large proportion of these men were in the field within a matter of days. The British Army could initially only muster around 100,000 men, who were promptly dubbed by Kaiser Wilhelm a 'contemptible little army'.

However, the British rapidly formed four infantry and one cavalry divisions and they were in France by 5 August, under the name of the British Expeditionary Force (BEF). Although well trained, with a deep understanding of the fieldcraft of war, they lacked the fire power of the enemy. Therefore British Army Field Marshal Lord Kitchener, of Second Boer War fame, was made Secretary of War and given the task of raising a new volunteer army, initially of 100,000, with more recruits to follow. As soon as the war started, the government began to produce propaganda material to urge the recruitment of volunteers and to maintain morale at home.

One of the most famous images of the war is the recruiting poster featuring a portrait of Kitchener, captioned 'Your Country needs you'. Another used the following poem by Edith B. Billman:

'Britain'
Brave sons of Britain!
Boys of the bull-dog breed!
Rally round the grand old flag
– it's you we need.
It is England – England
calling you today.
Arise! And smile the hateful traitor foe.
In guiltless blood, his hands are steeped, we know.
Now onward, Boys!
To strike the shattering blow.

There were many many more recruitment posters and they certainly played their part, as by December 1914 over one million volunteers had enlisted. By January 1915, one hundred men from the Salvation Army colony at Hadleigh alone had enlisted. In many cases, groups of men from the same factories and businesses joined up together, forming battalions known as 'Pals Battalions'. One of the authors' grandfathers, James Frederick Pitts, joined a Pals Battalion. The idea was first suggested by Lord Derby and it was reasonably successful, with a number of battalions formed across the country. The major drawback to the Pals Battalions though, was that many towns lost their entire population of military-age men in one stroke, when the battalions were involved in battles with particularly high losses. This, however, did not seem to affect the Castle Point area, as there was no large employer and therefore no local Pals Battalion was formed.

The war would not end by Christmas, as had been so confidently asserted, or even within the year. By January 1916, with increasing casualties and falling numbers of volunteers coming forward, the Government realised that over 600,000 men of eligible age had not yet volunteered and seemed unlikely to do so. In response to this the

Military Service Act was put in place, becoming law on 27 January 1916, and conscription came into being for the first time in British history. Initially it was intended only for physically able single men, aged between 18 and 41, but later married men were also conscripted and in 1918 the age limit was raised to 51. The act did exempt those who were not medically fit, as well as clergymen, teachers, widowers with children and those working in reserved occupations, such as war industries.

Conscription was not a very popular policy and in April 1916 over 200,000 people demonstrated against it in London's Trafalgar Square. However, it was extended after the war too, into 1920, to enable the army to deal with continuing trouble spots throughout the Empire and in Europe. There were four grounds on which individuals could apply for a certificate of exemption from conscription into the armed services:

> *If it is expedient in the national interests that he should be engaged in other work, or if he is being educated or trained for any other work, that he should continue; or if serious hardship would ensue owing to his exceptional financial or business obligations or domestic position; or ill health or infirmity; or conscientious objection to the undertaking of combatant service.*

Men seeking an exemption had to appeal, either on their own behalf or through their employer, to a local Military Service Tribunal in the town or district. Any applicant refused exemption by the Tribunal or dissatisfied with the type of exemption given, had the right of appeal. Conversely, military representatives or recruiting officers could also appeal against an exemption granted to an applicant. If either party was still dissatisfied they could appeal to a Central Tribunal, but only if this was allowed by the Appeals Tribunal.

The largest proportion of men seeking exemptions were conscientious objectors, individuals who claimed the right to refuse to perform military service on the grounds of freedom of thought, conscience or religion. They also had the right to go through the procedure as laid out above. By the end of the war around 7,000 men had been granted exemption on the basis that they would perform non-combatant duties, 3,000 more had been sent to special work camps, and 6,000 imprisoned. Another forty-two were sent to the Front to face a firing squad, although their sentences were immediately reprieved many of them faced ten years' penal servitude. Yet it would appear that few served for very long and most had been released by 1919.

On 30 June 1916, the *Chelmsford Chronicle* reported a speech by the Prime Minister, Herbert Asquith in which he revealed that a Home Office Committee had been appointed to determine what kind of work the 'genuine' conscientious objector could be put to. He went on to say, 'All men who honestly objected to military service ought to be able to avail themselves of Parliamentary exemption, but those guilty of the double offence of cowardice and hypocrisy would be treated with the utmost rigour.' Men held to be 'genuine' conscientious objectors would be released from civil prisons, on the condition of their performing work deemed of national importance.

It was not long before the Tribunals were receiving a flood of exemption application requests, and even the Church got involved.

> ### *Chelmsford Chronicle,* 14 April 1916:
> *The Vicar and Churchwardens of South Benfleet applied for the exemption of Ernest Albert Jennings, aged 29, sexton, clerk etc. South Benfleet – Mr H Beckett, one of the churchwardens, said the greatest difficulty was in finding a substitute to dig the graves – The Chairman said in other parishes a grave digger was borrowed. The application was refused.*

So off to war Ernest went, enlisting in the 1st Battalion, Essex Regiment, at the rank of private. The next piece of information about him to be reported in the *Chelmsford Chronicle*, on 16 February 1917, was that he had been killed in action on 16 January 1917. Ernest is buried at St Sever Cemetery Extension in Rouen, France.

The paper also reported that the same Tribunal also dealt with the following conscientious objector:

> *Murray Cecil Frost, decorator, etc., Hadleigh, aged 26, objected to military service on the ground that he was a Christadelphian. He had been against fighting since he was immersed last November. The Chairman: You are not willing*

to go into any non-combatant service? Applicant: I am not.
In answer to Colonel Newitt, applicant said there was no
conspiracy on the part of his elders to prevent them serving
their country. The tribunal refused the application.

It is not clear whether Murray Frost later enlisted, went to prison or ended up in a wartime factory, but he does not appear to have been living with his parents in 1918, according to the electoral register for Hadleigh. He survived the war and married Jessie Ham in 1924.

The *Chelmsford Chronicle* reported the case of another local conscientious objector on Friday 14 July 1916 :

Walter A Pease, 30, cowman, Daws Heath, employer Mr W
Thorington, Thundersley applied on conscientious grounds.
The Chairman said applicant was in reserved occupation
and could appeal on that ground. He agreed to do so.
Colonel Newitt: 'You are anxious to be a martyr?' The
applicant, 'I do not want to do any killing.'

The next case, reported in July 1916, was that of Harold Thorington, 28, a market gardener, from Daws Heath, who also applied on conscientious grounds. He was a member of the Peculiar People, a religious sect established in Essex in the mid-1800s. In the 1901 census the ten-year-old Thorington is recorded as living with his grandparents, and by 1911 he had joined the Peculiar People and begun attending their chapel at Daws Heath, Thundersley. He married Martha Whitwell in early 1914.

Harold's army record shows that he was recommended for non-combatant service on the grounds that he was a conscientious objector. At the Tribunal, Thorington said that before he gave his heart to God he was 'very handy with his fists.' He claimed that he had already sacrificed several weeks' employment for his conscience, because he would not attest. Thorington was granted non-combatant service. In October 1916, Harold Thorington also appealed against his non-combatant service. He repeated that he had held a conscientious objection to war since he was saved in 1906, and he was commanded by God to love his enemies. A member of the Tribunal, Mr E.C. Gray asked: 'Whom do you love?' Thorington replied: 'I love the Germans, they say they are my enemies.' He was not granted exemption and his case was dismissed.

Thorington appeared before the Rochford Magistrates on 26 October 1916, for failing to report to his army unit, the 9th Eastern Company Non-Combatant Corps and was fined £2, to be deducted from his army pay. He was then tried, convicted at a court martial and given 112 days' detention. What happened to him after this point has not been ascertained, although he did return home after the war.

Another member of the Peculiar People, James Smith, appealed in November 1914. James was a 39-year-old bricklayer from Daws Heath, Thundersley, and he appealed against non-combatant service on the basis that he had formerly believed in an eye for an eye and a tooth for a tooth, but he had renounced that doctrine when he was saved at the Peculiar People's Chapel in Southend, ten years previously. Smith's appeal was dismissed.

Unlike Smith and Thorington, Arthur G. Bearman, a 34-year-old married greengrocer from South Benfleet, appealed on medical and business grounds. Three years previously he had injured his head and spine in an accident. The local paper reported that the case was adjourned for a week, possibly while medical advice was sought. Arthur was born in 1883 and on the outbreak of war he was living at 'The Bungalow, The Avenue, Thundersley'. It would appear from his records that he attended the Southend recruitment office in January 1916 and completed the Short Service enlistment form, agreeing to serve his country. He was immediately transferred to the Army Reserve, but according to the report of his appeal it would appear that he had second thoughts.

Subsequent medical examination declared Arthur Bearman fit for active service, so he returned to his regiment, 'A' Company, 16th Battalion Essex Regiment Territorial Force, on 25 October 1916. He was, for a time, transferred to The Royal Army Service Corps (RASC), as a driver. The function of the RASC was to provide the fighting soldier with everything he needed to perform his task – food, water, ammunition, weapons – all had to be transported to men at the Front Line from a central point in the United Kingdom.

The RASC were the unsung heroes of the British Army. At its peak the Corps had 10,547 officers and 315,334 men plus tens of thousands of Colonial troops and labourers. The RASC got the nickname 'Ally

Sloper's Cavalry' after a comic book character who first appeared in 1867, in *Judy* magazine. Unlike the hardworking RASC, Sloper was a cheeky, slippery, conniving rogue who enjoyed a drink.

Their role of transporting provisions and equipment to the Front Line meant that men in the RASC would be attached to the various units of the army in each of the separate theatres of the war. Arthur remained at Base Depots in the United Kingdom for the first two years of his service, before going to France on 18 March 1917, returning home on 2 May 1919 and being demobbed the following day, He was awarded the Victory and British War Medals, plus a Good Conduct Badge.

On 13 October 1916, the *Chelmsford Chronicle* reported the appeals of two more Thundersley men: 'Frederick Stibbards, 36, builder and decorator, Thundersley, appealed for himself and also for Albert C James, 26, – both dismissed, a month being allowed in each case.' Frederick was living in Thundersley in 1918, so he may not have been conscripted, yet James seems to have disappeared from the area. However, another Stibbards, Albert from Hadleigh, also appeared in the paper when he applied for exemption in January 1917. Albert was born on 22 October 1885 at Hadleigh to Samuel and Ann, and it has not been confirmed whether he and Frederick were related. Albert's father had started up an undertakers business in the village in 1867.

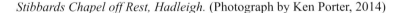

Stibbards Chapel off Rest, Hadleigh. (Photograph by Ken Porter, 2014)

The *Essex Newsman* of 27 January 1917 reported the following, under the heading 'The Only Undertaker':

> *Albert M Stibbards 30, wheelwright and undertaker, Hadleigh, asked for exemption on business grounds. His brother had been given conditional exemption by the Rochford Tribunal. He was the only undertaker in the district and conducted about two hundred funerals a year. It was impossible to get ready-made coffins. The Chairman said temporary exemptions for two months would be granted. They did that to enable appellant to make arrangements for obtaining already sawn timber and they did not hold out to him any prospect of success on a renewed application.*

Albert was back at the Tribunal in April and this time he pleaded a conscientious objection, explaining that he regarded war as wholesale murder. He would be no more justified in killing any member of the Tribunal than a German, he said. His application was rejected but he was sent for non-combatant service, rather than to the Front.

Albert enlisted in a Medical Corps attached to one of the local battalions. On his return, he rejoined his brother David in the family business and, in May 1921, following the death of their father, he took over the business. Albert also became a local Methodist preacher, a position he held for sixty years. The business survived and is still run by Martin Stibbards, the great-grandson of Albert's brother David. Albert passed away in December 1973.

At the same Tribunal where Albert Stibbards appealed, Albert H. Kearsey, 33, a storekeeper from Rayleigh Road, Thundersley, appealed on the grounds of ill-health. He had already been rejected after trying to enlist on five occasions. He explained that he had received a pink form and travelled to Warley, Essex, where he was passed fit for general service. The same day he saw a local doctor, who said that he feared Albert was developing tuberculosis.

At his Tribunal, a letter from Major Lawther, the commanding officer of the 4th Battalion Essex Volunteer Regiment, was read. In this letter, the Major called attention to Albert's poor physical condition. To put him in the army he wrote, would kill him. The medical

The Stibbards family grave, St James the Less Churchyard, Hadleigh.
(Photograph by Ken Porter, 2014)

examinations Albert had undergone at Warley seemed to be very cursory, in the Major's view. The case was referred to the Central Medical Board, who confirmed the Warley decision that Albert was fit for general service. It has not been possible to discover whether Albert went on to serve in the armed forces, but he was living with his wife Edith Helena in Thundersley at the time of the 1918 electoral register. He died in March 1965, aged eighty-one – not bad for someone suffering from severe ill-health at the age of thirty-three.

Like Albert Stibbards, Robert H.C. Nash, a forty-year-old cow keeper and dairyman from Hadleigh, argued that he should be exempt from military service as he was the only dairyman in that place. He was also married with five children and would turn forty-one on 13 February 1917. The Tribunal granted him exemption until his forty-first birthday, when he would be legally exempt. The 1918 electoral register for Hadleigh records Robert Nash living with his wife Adelaide at 'The Dairy' on Leigh Road, so presumably, he also managed to escape conscription.

Without the full transcript of each Tribunal appeal it is very difficult to understand how the various Tribunals came to their decisions. For example, in the case of a Benfleet grocer, the military tried on two occasions to get the original decision of exemption overturned This case was reported in the *Chemsford Chronicle* on 14 September 1917 and 23 November 1917:

> *The Military Representative applied for withdrawal of the certificate of H.W. P Marchant, 36, grocer, South Benfleet who stated that attached to his grocery trade he had an important corn business, which his wife and assistant could not possibly manage. Previous to the war he had three men who had all joined up. The military application was refused.*
>
> *The military then entered another appeal against the exemption granted by the Rochford Tribunal to Herbert W. P. Marchant, 37, grocer and provision merchant, of the Station stores, South Benfleet. The Rochford Tribunal considered that the applicant's work was of national importance in supplying foodstuffs. Replying to Captain Howard the applicant said he had, on account of shortness of staff, to give up some rounds. He had four horses and a van and delivered on to Canvey Island. His wife without his assistance could not carry on their business.*
>
> *The Chairman said the military appeal would be allowed. The Tribunal recognised that the supply of food to Canvey Island must be carried on, but they thought it ought not to be done by a general service man. Temporary exemption would be granted for three months for applicant to make other arrangements.*

According to these facts alone it seems a harsh decision, as the business might have gone to the wall and Marchant's wife would possibly have faced financial hardship.

'Saving Private Staines'

Compassion did not appear to be taken much into account in another case covered by the *Chelmsford Chronicle* on 14 September 1917, in which Leonard George Staines, aged twenty-nine, of South Benfleet, asked for temporary exemption. He told the Tribunal that he wished to apply for exemption because he had just lost his third brother in the war. The Tribunal refused the appeal but noted that Staines was not to be called up before 14 October.

The popular film *Saving Private Ryan* consists of the American military expending huge effort to try to save the last surviving brother among four servicemen during the Second World War. It would appear that Hadleigh had a similar story in the case of Leonard Staines, although there is a slightly different twist, in that Leonard was trying to save himself by appealing against conscription. It is hard to blame him, as his parents Charles and Louisa Staines had already lost three sons, and must have feared losing their last remaining son too.

The first Staines brother to lose his life during during the war was Sydney Charles Staines. Sydney was born in Hadleigh in 1893. He enlisted at Southend in November 1914 into the 5th Battalion, Coldstream Guards, with the rank of private. For some reason he never left British shores and died in hospital at Hammersmith on 16 April 1916.

The first Staines brother to be killed in action was the second eldest, Lance Corporal Wilfred James. He was born at Hadleigh in 1891 and went to Hadleigh Church School. On leaving school, Wilfred worked for several employers in the building trade and the 1911 census has his occupation listed as 'brick labourer', the same as his father. It is possible that they

Sydney Charles Staines. (Photograph from the *Southend Standard*)

were both working at the Salvation Army brick works or the nearby brick works at Benfleet.

Wilfred enlisted at Southend on 5 October 1914 into the 9th Royal Fusiliers (City of London Regiment). His training was carried out at Colchester and Codfod St Mary and after nine months' training he found himself at the Front in July 1915. The Codford area of Salisbury Plain housed a large training camp where tens of thousands of troops were trained, while waiting to be transferred to France. It also became a depot in 1916 for the men who had been evacuated from the Front Line and were not yet fit to return.

Wilfred's first piece of action was the Battle of Loos, which commenced on 25 September 1915 and ended on the 14 October 1915. It was the largest British offensive mounted on the Western Front during 1915. The British used gas for the first time and deployed their newly trained army units. Like numerous battles to follow, it ended in a form of stalemate, although British casualties were double those of the Germans: 59,247 compared to 26,000. Wilfred, however, came through unscathed.

After a brief period of leave, he returned to take part in the Battle of the Somme. On the first day of the battle, 1 July 1916, he was shot through the hand and then treated at the Mile End Military Hospital. He had another period of leave at home in Hadleigh, before returning in October 1916. He was wounded again, on 25 April 1917, this time by shrapnel in the neck and for a time he was treated by a Casualty Clearing Station, where he helped to bring in the wounded, discovering among them an old school friend. Then on 22/23 June 1917, while acting as a bomb-thrower in skirmishes that followed the Battle of Arras, he was killed.

His commanding officer, Second Lieutenant C. E. Watson wrote:

I deeply regret to inform you that your son was killed in action yesterday evening. I sincerely sympathise with you in your sad loss, especially as he was one of my best and bravest, steadiest and noblest. He feared nothing. Mercifully death was instantaneous, not lingering. I hope you will understand how difficult this is for me to write; but believe me when I say how I sincerely sympathise with you. This morning I had his body taken behind and buried properly.

Wilfred was initially buried at Monchy-Le-Preu, but later transferred to Vis-En-Artois British Cemetery in Haucourt. He was awarded the 1914/15 Star, Victory and British War Medals. His name appears on the Hadleigh War Memorial, St James the Less Church War Memorial and a special grave memorial in the churchyard.

'A Private'
This ploughman dead in battle slept out of doors
Many a frozen night and merrily
Answered staid drinkers, good bedmen and all bores:
'At Mrs Greenland's Hawthorn Bush,' said he,
'I slept.' None knew which bush. Above the town,
Beyond 'The Drover', a hundred spot the down

In Wiltshire. And where now at last he sleeps
More sound in France – that, too, he secret keeps.
(By Phillip Edward Taylor, killed at the Battle of Arras
on 9 April 1917)

Approximately two months later, Charles and Louisa's youngest son, Archie, was killed. Archie was born at Hadleigh in 1897 and, like Wilfred, he had attended the church school and was later employed as a 'Yard Man', presumably at the local timber yard. He enlisted with the 96th Siege Battalion, Royal Garrison Artillery at Southend on 18 October 1915, at the rank of gunner (Bombardier). The 96th Siege Battalion were equipped with heavy howitzers (9.2inch BL Mk1 Siege Howitzer), capable of firing 290lb high explosives shells over a distance of 10,000 yards, each gun weighing fourteen tons. These were often employed in destroying or neutralising the enemy artillery, as well as putting destructive fire down on strong points, dumps, stores, roads and railways behind enemy lines.

Archie embarked at Southampton with the 96th on 24 May 1916 and landed at Le Havre. There is no doubt that he was involved in plenty of action before he was killed by a shell on 14 August 1917, just prior to the major offensive at the Battle of Langemarck, (16–18 August), which was part of the second Allied attack of the Third Battle of Ypres. He had been promoted to Bombardier on 3 April 1917.

His senior officer, Major C. R. Sturges, wrote:

I am deeply grieved to have to inform you that your son Bombardier Archie Staines was killed in action this morning. His death was instantaneous and was the result of shock caused by a shell bursting close by. There was no mark on his body whatever and he will be buried this evening in the little cemetery near here. Your son was a most promising non-commissioned officer and was a great favourite with all of us. Please accept the deepest sympathy of myself and the rest of battery in your great loss.

Gunner Sid Wheeler, a close colleague, also wrote the following to the Staines family:

It is with the greatest sorrow that I have to write these few lines to let you know the sad news of that your son, Archie, was killed in action on the gun. We were firing at the time when a German Shell fell right amongst us, killing Archie and three others. But perhaps it will relieve you to know that he suffered no pain, for when we came to look we could find no wound of any kind on his body. It was the shock of the explosion that killed him, as he died instantly. He was given a decent burial in one of our cemeteries just behind the line this evening. This has been a great upset to me for Archie and I have been together since the battery was formed and he was one of my best chums. He was a great favourite and loved by all the section. We all send our deepest sympathy to you in our great loss.

Archie's body was later moved to Loos British Cemetery and, like his brother Wilfred, he appears on the Hadleigh war memorials. Archie was awarded the Victory and British War Medals. After losing three sons, there is little wonder that the Staines family did not want their one surviving son to join the services. It would appear that Leonard did manage to avoid joining the army, as he appears on the 1918 electoral register, still living in Hadleigh. The reason was not reported in the local paper, but it is hoped that the Tribunal chose to be compassionate to this family who had lost so much.

The *Chelmsford Chronicle* of 23 November 1917 reported the following:

In November 1917 a letter from the front prompted the military to ask for a review of the case of Percival Frederick John Skelton, 24, of Hart Road, Thundersley, employed by Mr J. J. Lincoln, contractor.

The County Tribunal granted conditional exemption in April 1916. Captain Howard said this case was again brought to his notice by a letter from a man at the Front. Mr Lincoln, replying to Captain Howard, said he dealt in under wood. A little was used for firewood but it was mostly used for making hurdles. He supplied hurdles to the farmers and faggots to the military. Witness farmed two hundred acres

Grave of Sydney Charles Staines and memorial to his brothers, at St James the Less, Hadleigh Churchyard. (Photograph by Ken Porter, 2014)

of land, of which eighty eight were arable. The respondent was engaged in carting the wood.

The Chairman said the age of a timber cutter, haulier and sawyer, to be in a certified occupation was 22.

Captain Howard (to Lincoln): You agree with this letter I have received from a private at the Front, saying it is rather too bad for a youngster like this to be out of the Army. Lincoln: I cannot agree with your point there. I must have a man to haul my wood and he understands hauling.

Captain Howard: Is there any truth in this statement in the letter? It says: 'His uncle laughs to think he has taken the rise out of you gentlemen'

Lincoln: That is not true. – Upon being given the letter to read, he said it was absurd to say that any old man could do the work.

Answering Mr H. J. Jefferies, who represented the respondent, witness said the man was engaged in exactly the same work as when the Tribunal granted exemption in April 1916. The War Agricultural Committee recommended that the man was better left in his present employment.

The Chairman said the Tribunal did not think the man was in a certified occupation. They did not think he was a timber haulier in that sense of the word and no doubt he was chiefly employed in carting copse wood. No doubt he was very usefully employed. They could not send this young man into the army at the present time but it was the imperative duty of the employer to exhaust every possible means that lay in his power to the satisfaction of the Tribunal if an extension of time was applied for. Temporary exemption would be granted for two months.

There is no evidence that Skelton joined up, other than his absence from the 1918 electoral register for Thundersley.

Arthur Dedman, a farm worker from Canvey Island, was less successful in his appeal. On 19 August 1916, the *Essex Newsman* reported that Dedman's appeal for exemption had been dismissed and he was required to report for duty at the end of September. He had previously reported at Southend in January that year and completed the necessary papers, but as he was then not yet nineteen he had been asked to report back at a latter date. In the meantime he attempted to get an exemption.

Arthur Dedman eventually enlisted as a private in the 3rd Battalion, Essex regiment on 25 October 1916. After the required training, he was sent to Alexandria, joining the Egyptian Expeditionary Force (EEF) on 9 May 1917. During the Third Battle of Gaza on 3 November 1917, while fighting against troops from the Ottoman Empire he received a bayonet wound to his left knee. On 7 December 1917, the *Chelmsford Chronicle* reported that Dedman had also been wounded by a gunshot to the chest, and he was back in hospital in October 1918 through illness, just before the Armistice, not rejoining his unit until 2 February 1919. He was eventually discharged and transferred to the Z Army Reserve on 31 August 1919.

Most Tribunals were hostile towards applicants they believed were not genuine, and towards conscientious objectors. Press reports of the interviews between Tribunal members and the objectors often indicated a great gulf in understanding between the two. The results of these interviews were usually completely inconclusive, with Tribunal members none the wiser about the applicants' real motives other than their desire not to go to war.

The Tribunals showed particularly scant sympathy towards applicants who were revealed to be in any way dishonest. A classic case was reported in the *Essex County Standard*, on May 1917. Sidney Howard, a sand and gravel merchant from Thundersley, claimed that as a member of the Peculiar People, he felt that he could take no part in the war, which he believed was not of Christ, but of Satan.

> *In questioning Captain Howard asked 'You took these views after the war started'. Response 'Yes'.*
> *'What did you belong to before?'*
> *Response: 'I belonged to the devil then.'*
> *'Who was your employer then?'*
> *Response: 'He was.' (Laughter).*
> *'The devil? In what way was he?' (again Laughter).*
> *The appellant further stated that he did not feel that he wanted to die for his country.*

Captain Howard continued: 'Then die for your Saviour to endeavour to right wrong ...
The chairman in summing up said: 'We are not satisfied with your bona fides. You must go for full service.'

These are just a small sample of the thousands of people who refused to go to war, because they did not want to fight, were required for vital war work or were able to prove that their business would suffer without them. Those applying for an exemption often went to some lengths to convince the Tribunals that they were needed at home. Yet many whose applications were turned down and who were subsequently forced to join the services turned out to be heroes, including some former conscientious objectors.

A few soldiers changed their minds about serving halfway through their time in the military, and deserted after they came home on leave. The *Essex Newsman* reported on 24 August 1918, barely three months before the end of the war, that Mrs Rose Passfield of High Street, Hadleigh, had been summoned for concealing a deserter. It would appear that her son-in-law Wallace Henry Francis Church had turned up at her house a fortnight ago, saying he had two days' leave from the Essex Regiment.

Church was arrested at the house as a deserter by a Sgt Perry and PC Ponder. The bench sentenced the defendant to one month's imprisonment, although he protested, 'I have five children at home; can't you make it a fine?' The Chairman refused. Mrs Passfield and her husband Joseph had been in a difficult situation. Should they have notified the authorities and turned in their son-in-law?

Essex Newsman reported the case of another local soldier who outstayed his leave in August 1915, yet this time the outcome was far more tragic. Rifleman Charles Percy Culliford of the 12th (County of London) Battalion (The Rangers) was found on the Midland Railway between Leigh and South Benfleet, after his head had been cut off by a train. Private T. R. Hawkins, of the South Staffordshire Regiment, then stationed at Canvey Island, told the coroner that he had seen the deceased on the island near the Creek on Sunday night.

Culliford had been in full uniform and told Hawkins he had come from London. He walked with his head down and he had a worried look. Other witnesses saw him walking along the line towards Leigh and when he was found, his tunic and belt were lying nearby on the bank. At the inquest the jury returned a verdict of suicide while of unsound mind.

War Horses

Another factor that would affect everyday life in Britain during the war was the army's need for horses, which were still a major form of transport for people living in more rural areas. The army required horses not only for the cavalry, but also to transport the guns and supplies, as vehicles easily became stuck in the mud.

The 2011 film *War Horse* gives an idea of the appalling conditions that the army horses, ponies and mules had to deal with during the war. Their story begins with the mass call-up of horses from every farm and country estate in the land, but between 1914 and 1918 the British Army would take over 1,000,000 horses to war. The first clash between the cavalry horse and the machine gun was terrible. Although the horses and the cavalry men who rode them had gone through a period of training, there was no way any form of training could match the devastating fire power of the machine gun and artillery shells. It was chaotic right from the outset, with horses and men tumbling and falling in every direction at the Battle of Mons.

Although used only infrequently, cavalry charges continued and the last attack was at the Battle of the Somme on 14 July 1916, at High Wood. This attack proved costly, with 102 men killed along with 130 horses. It was not long before the British public became very concerned about the welfare of horses at the Front and the sudden dearth of horses and ponies at home. As early as November 1914 the Essex papers were expressing concern about the situation. On 27 November 1914, the *Chelmsford Chronicle* reported:

WAR HORSES AND HUNTING

In the last issue of 'Country Life' a number of authorities expressed the opinion that there is a grave shortage of horses in this country. Sir Walter Gilbey considers that (1) no more mares should be sent out of the country and (2) mares of any value that have been too seriously injured at the front should be shipped back home for breeding purposes. Captain Godfrey Heseltine holds that the

Government at present, by introducing a Bill to make M.F.H.'s (Master Fox Hunts) liable for poultry losses by Law, are putting the last nail in the coffin of fox-hunting. Unless the Government are prepared to start large breeding establishments of their own, the death of fox-hunting will assuredly entail the end of light horse breeding.

Horses were desperately needed at the Front, according to the *Chelmsford Chronicle* of 13 August 1915:

HORSES FOR THE ARMY

Lord Selborne, President of the Board of Agriculture and Fisheries, after consultation with the Chairman of the Advisory Council on Light Horse breeding, has appointed a committee to consider and advise the Board what steps should be taken to secure the production and maintenance in England and Wales of a supply of horses suitable and sufficient for military purposes especially on mobilisation.

Then, in 1917, the *Chelmsford Chronicle* reported the following story under the headline, 'Horses Were More Precious Than Gold':

At the Harwich Tribunal on Monday exemption was claimed for a scavenger. The applicant said the man looked after five horses and two-year-olds were fetching seventy to eighty guineas. They wanted looking after. They were more precious than gold to-day. – The individual obviously made his point and he was given a conditional exemption.

Soldiers too were concerned; Gunner Pamlin of Walthamstow wrote home in November 1914 about the plight of army horses:

Here are exciting times of Tuesday 1 September: 'reveille at 2.30. Saddle and harness up but the order was passed down to water horses, in a quarter of an hour. The Battery had all watered except No. 6, who were then at water, when at 5.50 a.m. the camp was surprised by Germans. The enemy had ten guns and a squadron of Uhlans, with infantry and maxims. The first round stampeded the horses and the whole forces opened fire. Every horse was riddled and the whole camp was soon wrecked. The sight was terrible. Legs and arms, horses and men, blown to fragments.

Even senior soldiers spoke out, like Brigadier General Frank Percy Crozier, who took part in various battles on the Western Front. Crozier had this to say in his publication, *A Brass Hat in No Man's Land* (1930): 'If times are hard for human beings, on account of the mud and misery which they endure with astounding fortitude, the same may be said of the animals. My heart bleeds for the horse and mules.'

The 1914 Defence of the Realm Act

On 8 August 1914, three days after the Alien Restriction Act was implemented, the Defence of the Realm Act (DORA) was passed. It gave the Government wide-ranging powers to control the lives of the civilian population and if any laws were broken people could be swiftly prosecuted. The Act restricted British civilians in the following ways:

- Talking about naval or military matters in public places was prohibited, as was spreading rumours about military matters.
- Binoculars were no longer to be sold.
- Trespassing on railway lines and bridges was strictly forbidden.
- Melting gold and silver was banned.
- No one was allowed to light bonfires or fireworks.
- Food wastage, for instance giving bread to horses or chickens, was prohibited.
- Correspondents were not allowed to use invisible ink when writing abroad.
- Brandy and whisky were no longer sold in railway refreshment rooms.
- Church bells were silenced for the duration of the war.

The Act also gave the Government increased powers, allowing them to:

- Take over any factory or workshop for wartime production.
- Try any civilian for breaking these new laws.

- Seize any land needed for military purposes. Censor newspapers and other media.

As the war continued and evolved, the Government introduced more clauses to DORA, including the introduction of British Summer Time, to provide more daylight hours for farmers. Publicans suffered as their opening hours were cut, their beer was watered down and customers were not allowed to buy rounds of drinks.

Although many of these regulations appear extremely trivial, they were brought in to help prevent a German invasion and to attempt to keep morale at home high. Preventing families from flying kites or lighting bonfires might seem a little strange, but it was deemed that these activities could potentially attract Zeppelins. Far more troubling for most Britons on the Home Front was the dwindling working male population, especially for employers. Before the war, many forms of employment had been closed to women and, once married, a large proportion were restricted to domestic work. The war would soon change that.

Thousands of women responded enthusiatically to the appeal for workers, taking over many jobs previously done only by men. They moved in greater numbers than ever before on to the farms, into munition factories, transport industry, banking, civil service etc – wherever there was a need. At least one million more women joined the British workforce between 1914 and 1918. In July 1915, David Lloyd George said that 'without women, victory will tarry.'

In addition, over 80,000 women had volunteered for some form of war service and another 100,000 served as professional nurses or volunteer nurses, known as VADs (Voluntary Aid Detachment). As the VADs obviously lacked the skills of the professionally trained nurses, they were initially restrict to working in hospitals in the United Kingdom. As the war progressed and their skill and efficiency levels improved, along with the growing shortage of trained nurses, VADs were allowed to work overseas in military hospitals. They found themselves near the Western Front, Mesopotamia, Gallipoli and the Eastern Front and many were decorated for distinguished service.

At the beginning of the war, civilians on the Home Front saw men disappearing from town and city streets into the forces. They experienced the fear of invasion and spy hysteria, and learned that

German bombs could reach British shores. Women saw their employment opportunities widen, as they began working in once male-dominated industries, whilst Britons griped about having many of their former basic liberties undercut by DORA.

Even the hours of daylight were changed, with the introduction of 'Summer Time'. The idea behind this measure was to create more daylight, to help businesses preserve fuel but at the time it was very confusing for the populus. However, at least one person was happy with the idea: the author of the following poem.

> **'A Happy Hour'**
> *I must bid goodbye to Summer time.*
> *Which has been such a boon to me.*
> *And that extra hour in the garden*
> *In the evening after tea.*
> *I shall miss the daylight sadly*
> *When it comes to Monday night*
> *And sixty minutes earlier*
> *My lamp I'll need to light.*
> *But, happy though I can alter the clock*
> *Without grieving about the past.*
> *For I shall recover that hour's sleep*
> *Which I lost in April last.*
> (Author unknown, published in the
> *Dover Express,* 14 September 1917.)

Despite these changes people still managed to carry on as normally as possible and also involved themselves in various activities and fundraising drives to help the war effort, such as the Essex Regiment's Prisoners of War Fund. It was reported in 1917 that the fund was now sending food parcels to over 300 men, each costing about £2 2s a month. The fund was based on a process by which each parish adopted its own prisoners. Hadleigh was one of these areas and the organisers looked for people to come forward and adopt a prisoner. As late as September 1918, the Benfleet Scouts held a fête in the vicarage grounds and raised £30 for the fund.

Other charities also received local support. For instance, Canvey Island Parish Council donated £3 to the Prince of Wales's Relief Fund.

Concerts were also arranged on Canvey Island for wounded soldiers who had been transferred there. The Hadleigh Ladies' War Distress and Belgian Committee produced 200 garments for the poor of Hadleigh in 1915 and sent about 630 garments to the Belgian refugees.

Many people sprang to action in August 1914, like the Rochford parish guardian who, representing Thundersley, telegraphed to his Board asking for the loan of forty old bedsteads for the wounded, if and when they were required. 'Stand by, all to your posts for King and Country,' he added.

On 22 January 1915, 120 Belgian soldiers were entertained for tea and a musical evening, at the invitation of Mr W.H. Sheridan of Thundersley, and after the tea each man received a gift of cigarettes and matches. In fact, as early as November 1914 Hadleigh was playing host to a large number of convalescent Belgian soldiers, whose health was improving so rapidly that the parish council felt obliged to tighten up the local licensing hours.

When war broke out there were street celebrations throughout Great Britain but, as we now know, this enthusiasm did not last. After the Retreat from Mons, followed by the Battle of the Marne on 6–10 September 1914, it became obvious that there would be no quick overall victory. When at last October 1918 arrived, and it appeared that after four years of uphill fighting and grappling against tremendous odds, the war would soon be over, many must have felt amazed, even numb, after all they had endured and lost

CHAPTER 4

The War at Sea

As a young boy, Prince Wilhelm, the future Kaiser Wilhelm II, had been impressed by the Royal Navy on visits to see his grandmother, Queen Victoria, and his cousins. Later in life, he realised that if Germany was to match Britain's dominance, then Germany must construct a fleet to match its rival's.

To maintain its dominance, at the beginning of the twentieth century the British Admiralty believed that the navy would need to be larger than the next two biggest navies put together, although it was soon evident that this would not be viable, so they settled for a 60 per cent margin. As early as 1906, the First Sea Lord, John Fisher, began drawing up plans for a naval war against Germany. He reportedly told the Prince of Wales, 'Germany keeps her whole fleet concentrated within a few hours of England. We must therefore keep a fleet twice as powerful within a few hours of Germany.' By 1909 it had become obvious that the German Navy was catching up. The British Government had planned four new battleships but, as Winston Churchill put it, 'The Admiralty had demanded six new ships; the economist offered four; and we finally compromised on eight.'

The predominant design of battleships being built by the British in the lead up to the First World War was based on HMS *Dreadnought*, which was launched in 1906. The design had two main new features, an 'all-big-guns' feature, being a main battery of ten 12-inch guns, whereas the *Dreadnought*'s closest competitors carried only four guns. The second feature was steam turbine propulsion, giving the ship a capability of 21 knots, a speed that eclipsed the capabilities of earlier types of battleships. Subsequent battleships, both British and German, were commonly know as 'dreadnoughts'.

Another type of ship built just before the war was the battlecruiser. The design was very similar to that of the heavier dreadnoughts, but it lacked armour to save weight in order to improve speed. The German design kept its heavy armour but reduced the size of the guns to help gain the extra speed. Then there were the torpedo boat destroyers or simple destroyers, which were capable in large numbers of overwhelming a single dreadnought. Finally, there were the submarines or U-boats, which were more effective in attacking poorly defended merchant ships than in combat with surface warships, although they did sink several British warships at the beginning of the war.

Although the focus of the First World War was on the Western Front, the war at sea was also critical. As Winston Churchill, who had been made First Lord of the Admiralty in 1911, indicated, whoever controlled the high seas was more likely to win the war. Fortunately, during 1914-1918 there was only one major battle at sea, The Battle of Jutland, which ended in stalemate and another two significant engagements, the Battles of Dogger Bank and Heligoland Bight. Although the Royal Navy suffered greater losses and casualties it did achieve its main objective of ensuring that the German fleet stayed in port for the major part of the war.

This enabled the Royal Navy to provide extra protection for Britain's merchant ships against the German submarine attacks and to blockade German ports, restricting their ability to receive overseas supplies and resources. This was one of the main factors that resulted in Germany requesting a ceasefire at a time when they appeared close to winning the war.

Being an island nation, Britain was also heavily reliant on imports from overseas. So the German Navy used U-boats in its attempt to blockade Britain. U-boats sank hundreds of Allied merchant ships, resulting in many civilian deaths when there were passengers on board. In 1917, Germany declared unrestricted submarine warfare, including attacks made without any warning against all ships in the 'war zone'. The problem of U-boat attacks was eventually overcome by grouping merchant ships together in convoys, so that they could be more easily defended.

HMS Aboukir. (Postcard)

Canvey Islanders Aboard the *Aboukir*

One of the major concerns for the British Admiralty was to keep control of the English Channel, as it was the major artery for the British Expeditionary Force (BEF) to transport supplies, troops and casualties. The British decided not to station any large warships in the Channel, because they were required to keep the German High Seas Fleet under control in the North Sea. This was clearly a successful ploy, as the Channel was never attacked directly by the German High Seas Fleet.

The British Admiralty had an early scare when, on 22 September 1914, three Royal Navy Cruisers, HMS *Aboukir*, HMS *Hogue* and HMS *Cressy,* were torpedoed and sunk by a German submarine, *Unteressboot U-9*, commanded by Kapitanleutnant Otto Weddigen, about 40 miles off the Hook of Holland. The three ships, along with sister ships *Bacchante* and *Euryalus*, were old Cressy-class armoured cruisers and shortly after the outbreak of war they had been assigned to the 7th Cruiser Squadron. Their role was to support a force of destroyers and submarines to patrol the area of the North Sea known as the Broad Fourteens, to ensure that German warships could not attack the supply route in the Channel. These were old ships badly in need of repairs; worn out by the start of the war they could only manage about 15 knots. Each of the ships had over seven hundred officers and men and a handful of cadets, who were mostly aged under fifteen.

Amongst the naval hierarchy there was some opposition to these ships being used for this purpose, on the grounds that they would be vulnerable to a raid by more modern German warships. Because of this the patrol was nicknamed the 'live boat squadron'. On 20 September the ships, (excluding HMS *Bacchante*), were preparing to go on patrol under Rear Admiral Christian in HMS *Euryalus*. However, *Euryalus* had to drop out due to the lack of coal and the Rear Admiral was unable to transfer to another ship due to appalling weather conditions, which also kept the destroyers in port.

Command was delegated to Captain John Drummond on *Aboukir*. After weeks of daily patrols, the ships' old engines could not manage to maintain even the steady 15 knots they had previously managed and their speed dropped dramatically to 12 and sometimes 9 knots. To try and maintain as much speed as possible they had to resort to zigzagging, making it easier for them to be attacked.

Just after 6:00 on 22 September, the German submarine *U-9*, under the command of Otto Weddigen, sighted the three ships steaming in line at about 10 knots. Weddigen ordered his submarine to submerge, so that he could get closer to the unsuspecting ships. At a range of about 550 yards he fired a torpedo at *Aboukir* which struck her on the port side, breaking her back. She sank within twenty minutes, with the loss of 527 men.

Initially, Captain Drummond and the captains of the other two ships, *Cressy* and *Hogue*, thought the *Aboukir* had struck a floating mine and came forward to assist her. Captain Drummond soon realised that she had been torpedoed and ordered the ships away, but it was too late. Meanwhile, thinking that he was on the side of *Aboukir* facing away from the submarine, Captain Nicholson of the *Hogue* had stopped his ship to pick up survivors, but *U-9* had manoeuvred to the other side. From a distance of 300 yards it fired two torpedoes which hit the *Hogue* midship. It took just over ten minutes for her to sink.

U-9 then turned on the *Cressy*, which had also stopped to pick up survivors, and fired two torpedoes at the *Cressy*, at a range of about 1,000 yards. One hit *Cressy* on her starboard side and the other missed,

Shell from HMS Aboukir. (With kind permission of Bay Museum, Canvey Island)

but *U-9* then closed down on her and at 500 yards fired her last torpedo, which proved fatal. The *Cressy* sank within half an hour. Survivors were picked up by a number of nearby merchant ships, including the Dutch *Flora* and *Titan* and the British trawlers *JGC* and *Coriander*, before a Harwich force of light cruisers and destroyers arrived.

HMS Hogue. (Postcard)

Although 837 men were rescued, 1,459 died during the sinking of the three vessels.

The *Chelmsford Chronicle* reported the news under the heading, 'The Naval Reverse':

Canvey Island is greatly concerned as to the fate of several men who were serving on the Aboukir, viz., Arthur Jennings and Alfred Bond, stokers, both married; and Adolphus Smith, 1st class signaller, unmarried. On the Hogue was William Easterbrook, who with Bond, represented the local Coastguard Services on these ships.

South-East Essex Casualties on the *Aboukir, Cressy* and *Hogue*:
Arthur Jennings' grandfather Robert Jennings brought his family to Canvey Island around 1870. His father Charles married Emma King in 1883, and Arthur was born on 22 October 1885. Six years later, the census records that Arthur and his parents were living in the village, next to the local post office. His naval records reveal that he signed up on 23 November 1903, at the age of seventeen, for a twelve-year period as a stoker.

Arthur went on to serve on a number of ships, and his longest stretch was with HMS *Pathfinder* from 1906–1910, defending British territorial waters with the Home Fleet. In 1910 he bought himself out by transferring to the Royal Fleet Reserves. On the outbreak of war, he was called-up and joined HMS *Aboukir* on 2 August 1914. He was a Stoker First Class when he died at the age of twenty-seven. He is commemorated on the Canvey Island War Memorial, the memorial plaque in St Nicholas Church in Canvey and on the Chatham Naval Memorial.

Arthur is also listed in *De Ruvigny's Roll of Honour 1914-1918*. (The Marquis De Ruvigny's intention was to produce a biographical listing of every serviceman killed in the First World War, but this was not possible. However, the publication does feature biographies of over 26,000 deceased servicemen of all ranks and 7,000 photographs.)

Adolphus Smith was born on 11 December 1886 in Lowestoft, yet his parents Samuel and Emily were married on 27 September 1884 at the Parish Church on Canvey Island. Emily had been born on Canvey in 1864 and Samuel worked as a coastguard on Canvey Island, but soon after their marriage the couple moved to Suffolk. Samuel was invalided out of the Coastguards in 1894 and he died soon afterwards. Emily moved her children back to Canvey Island, to be near her family and married a local man, John Sorrell, in 1897.

Samuel was a career sailor, having signed up with the navy as a boy cadet in 1872, before changing to the Coastguards in 1881, so it must have come as no surprise to his family when Adolphus decided to follow suit, also joining the navy as a boy cadet in 1902, for a twelve-year period. In 1904, at the age of eighteen, he became a signalman. He was initially stationed at various land-based ships and training ships, before spending two years on HMS *Cadmus* on the China Station deployment between 1908 and 1910. The China Station was an area covering the Indian Ocean, the coast of China and its navigable rivers, in which the navy often co-operated with British commercial interests.

On 14 July 1914 Adolphus joined HMS *Aboukir* as a leading signalman; and one of his last acts would be to signal the ship's demise. Adophus is commemorated on the Canvey War Memorial and on the Chatham Naval Memorial. His mother Emily Sorrell was living at 12 Mill Cottages in Fobbing at the time of his death. He also appears in *De Ruvigny's Roll of Honour*.

William Thomas Easterbrook appears on the Canvey War Memorial, but he was born at Heaton, in Devon, to William and Jane Easterbrook on 22 March 1884. By the time of the 1901 census he had spent nearly two years as a boy cadet at the Royal Naval Barracks in Devonport. He was a coastguard at Canvey Island, before becoming an ordinary seaman when he joined the navy on 22 March 1902. He then served on many different ships, mostly training, gunnery and depot ships, until he joined HMS *Hogue* on 1 August 1914. He is also commemorated on the Plymouth Naval Memorial.

Stanley Moor Chiles was born on 9 April 1885 in Holborn, London, to Mary and Walter Chiles. The 1911 census notes that he was stationed on HMS *Flora*, at the rank of able seaman. The *Flora* was an Astraea, second class cruiser, built in 1893 and she was on the China Station at the time of the census, returning home in 1913. These particular cruisers were obsolete by the beginning of the war and so they were mainly used for training purposes. Stanley probably transferred from *Flora* to HMS *Aboukir* in 1913.

At the time of Stanley's death, his father was living at 'Hidaville' in Melcombe Road, South Benfleet, his mother having passed away.

He is commemorated on the Chatham Naval Memorial and South Benfleet Memorial.

John Henry Coolledge appears on the Hadleigh War Memorial despite the fact that he was born in Purleigh, Essex, on 25 July 1882 to Job and Sarah Coolledge. Prior to joining the navy, he was engaged by the Southend Waterworks Co. as a driver at their Pitsea pumping station. He joined the navy in September 1902 and married Alice Harriet Carey in 1911 at Leigh on Sea. His rank was that of Leading Stoker when he lost his life at the age of thirty, during the sinking of HMS *Cressy*. In addition to appearing on the Hadleigh War Memorial, he is also commemorated on the Chatham Naval Memorial and in *De Ruvigny's Roll of Honour*, which includes a photograph of him.

All five of these naval heroes were entitled to the 1914 Star, Victory and British War Medals.

On 16 October 1914, the *Chelmsford Chronicle* reported the following memorial service:

> *On Sunday evening a memorial service was held at St Katherine's Church, Canvey Island in memory of the gallant men who went down in the Hogue and Aboukir. In addition to the usual congregation there were assembled representatives of various bodies and members of the Police Force and Foresters.*
>
> *The navy was represented by the Chief Officer of Coastguard at Wakering. The names of the men in whose memory the service was held are: William Easterbrook, H.M.S, Hogue; Arthur Jennings, H.M.S. Aboukir and Adolphus Smith, H.M.S. Aboukir. The Vicar, the Rev. Joseph R Brown, was the preacher, taking for his text the 13th verse, Chapter 16, 1st Corinthians: 'Quit you like men.' Throughout the sermon he emphasised the heroic manner in which the men had gone to their doom. They had quitted themselves like men.*

Alfred Bond was one of the survivors of the sinking of HMS *Aboukir* and by 1918 he had returned to the Coastguard Station on Canvey Island.

Otto Eduard Weddigen, U-boat U-9. (Postcard)

Otto Eduard Weddigen was the commander of the *U-9* which sank the three British cruisers. At the time he was thirty-two years of age and had been in the German Navy for the past five years. He had married his childhood sweetheart on 16 August 1914, rejoining his submarine the next day, with the knowledge that there was a good chance he would soon be making his new wife a widow.

The following reminiscence was written by Weddigen, recalling the sinking of the three British vessels:

> *I set out from a North Sea port on one of the arms of the Kiel Canal and set my course in a south-westerly direction. Thus I was soon cruising off the coast of Holland. I had been lying in wait there only a few days before the morning of 22 September arrived, the day on which I fell in with my quarry.*

Weddigen had sighted several British ships during his passage, but he was after bigger prey. He travelled mainly on the surface, only submerging when he sighted ships. He was 18 sea miles north west of the Hook of Holland when, around 6:10, he sighted one of the big cruisers and soon afterwards two others. He was in a good position to let off his torpedoes but he decided to get closer, to make sure he would not miss.

> *I soon reached what I regarded as a good shooting point. I then let loose one of my torpedoes at the middle ship. I discovered that the shot had gone straight and true striking the ship under one of her magazines, which in exploding helped the torpedo's work of destruction. I later learned that the ship was the Aboukir.*

His memoirs go on to say: 'Her crew were brave and even with death staring them in the face kept to their posts, ready to handle their useless guns.' Once Weddigen's work was done he set course for home, reaching port on the following afternoon, where he found out that the news of his efforts had become public. He learned that his crew had won the approval of the Kaiser and they were to receive the Iron Cross, Second Class and he the Iron Cross, First Class.

This was Germany's first kill at sea, costing the Royal Navy three ships and 1,459 men. Otto went on to have further success: on 15 October 1914 he sunk HMS *Hawke*, with the loss of 527 men; on 12 March 1915 he sank a further three British ships, the *Andalusian*, *Indian City* and *Headlines*, luckily with no loss of life.

He later transferred to *U-29* and on 15 March 1915, while on patrol at Pentland Firth, Scotland, he surfaced and, after firing at HMS *Neptune*, he was rammed by HMS *Dreadnought*. The *U-29* sank, taking Weddigen and all his crew to their deaths.

The Battle of Jutland

Despite initial losses at sea, and the Allied forces being driven back in Belgium and France, after a few months of fighting the situation was slowly stabilising on the Western Front and the Royal Navy was gaining a stranglehold in the North Sea. As the months went by the Germans realised that they had to break this stranglehold. They knew that they did not have the numerical strength to win a head-to-head clash, though; for example they had 16 Dreadnought-class battleships but the Royal Navy had 28. The Germans therefore tried to adopt a divide and conquer strategy.

Their intention was to stage raids in the North Sea and bombard the English Coast, then try and lure out a few British ships at a time and pick them off. On 25 April 1916 the German Admiralty also decided to stop indiscriminate attacks by submarines on merchant shipping and deploy them against military ships instead. They hoped that such action might tempt the Royal Navy to engage in aggressive action, allowing them to lure the British Fleet into positions where they could be ambushed and destroyed. The Germans also intended to use Zeppelins, but were thwarted when the Russians obtained the main German code book from SMS *Magdeburg*, which had run aground in Russians waters. They passed it on to the Allies and it enabled the British to intercept and decrypt German signals.

It became obvious by late May 1916 that Germany was planning a major operation, so on 28 May the British Admiralty ordered all ships to be ready. Their rendezvous point was to be west of Skagerrak off the coast of Jutland. On 31 May, the first German battlecruiser was spotted and over the next few hours the two fleets engaged each other twice, with 250 ships involved: 151 British and 99 German. The Battle of Jutland was tactically inconclusive, though the Germans claimed victory on the basis that they sank 14 British ships (113,300 tons) killing 6,094 men against 11 ships (62,300 tons) with 2,551 killed. However, they were not able to break the British control of the North Sea, which was maintained throughout the war.

South-East Essex Sailors Lost at Sea in the Great War:
John French (also referred to as Jack) was born in Thundersley on 23 November 1878 to George and Harriet French. He was a Leading Stoker on board HMS *Formidable* when it was sunk by two torpedoes on 1 January 1915. He was thirty-eight years of age and he left a widow, Annie, as well as a son, John, and daughter, Lottie. In addition to being commemorated on the Hadleigh War Memorial, John French is also listed on the Chatham Naval Memorial.

HMS *Formidable* was the lead ship of her class of pre-dreadnought battleships. At the beginning of the war she was part of the 5th Battle Squadron based at Portland. She was assigned to defend the English Channel and was involved in seeing the British Expeditionary Force to France in August 1914. After a short spell at Sheerness, she once again returned to Portland and while on patrol she was struck by a torpedo from *U-24* at 2:20 on 1 January 1915.

At first it was thought that the *Formidable* might reach port, but twenty minutes later the captain gave the order to abandon ship. Then, at 10.01am she was struck again by a second torpedo on the starboard side. Although two light cruisers managed to get alongside and take on board survivors, she capsized and rolled over on to many of the men in the water. Of the 780 men on board, 512 men and 35 officers, including the captain and his dog, were drowned.

According to Nigel Clarke in the *Shipwreck Guide to Dorset and South Devon* (2008), there is a legendary twist to the story of HMS *Formidable*. After the wreck, the landlord of the Pilot Boat public house in the port of Lyme Regis offered its cellar as a makeshift mortuary. When the bodies had been laid out on the stone floor the publican found his cross-bred collie dog Lassie licking the face of one of bodies, nuzzling up against it to warm it with her fur. To the astonishment of everybody, Able Seaman John Cowan eventually stirred. He was taken to hospital and made a full recovery, later returning to the Pilot Boat to thank the dog for saving his life. The story, which was told time and time again, was eventually turned into the famous Hollywood 'Lassie' films.

George William Ross was born in 1891 at Woolwich. By the time of the 1911 census he was working as a civil employment clerk at the Stock Exchange and living with his father Thomas and three sisters at 'The Wharf' in South Benfleet High Street. He enlisted on 4 August 1914 into the Royal Naval Volunteer Reserves (RND) and was allocated to the Benbow Battalion. He was promoted to temporary sub-lieutenant on 7 January 1915 and joined the Howe Battalion in February 1915.

The RND was known as 'Winston's Little Army', as it was formed of excess men who had signed up for the Royal Navy. Howe Battalion was part of the 2nd Brigade, along with *Hood*, *Nelson* and *Anson*. It would appear they landed in Gallipoli sometime in April 1915 and two months later George Ross was killed, on 4 June 1915. His Commanding Officer wrote: 'Lieutenant Ross was badly wounded whilst in charge of a gun. Owing to heavy enemy fire, the order was

Trenches at Gallipoli. (Postcard)

given for the company to retire. Being unable to save the gun he destroyed it before retiring. Badly wounded in both arms and legs he dragged on behind at a distance of five yards when a shell burst and killed him.'

George is commemorated on the Helles Memorial in Turkey and the Southend on Sea Roll of Honour. He was awarded the 1914-15 Star, Victory and British War Medals.

Harold George Smith was born on 16 October 1880 at Bromley. He joined the navy at fifteen and the 1901 census shows that he was serving as an able seaman on HMS *Terrible*. Harold had, of course, seen action with the cruiser, which had provided landing parties in the relief of the Siege of Ladysmith in the Second Boer War. Soon afterwards, HMS *Terrible* found itself in the China Station and was stationed at Weihaiwei, a province on the eastern boarder of China

HMS Terrible. (Postcard)

leased by Britain (1898–1930) and while there, the ship was involved in suppressing the Boxer Rebellion.

Harold later served on the destroyers HMS *Speedy*, HMS *Skate* and HMS *Roebuck*. By the time of the 1911 census, he had retired from the navy and was living with his wife Isabella and young daughter, Hilda, at East Ham. On the outbreak of war he was called up as a reservist, serving on HMS *Sutlej* and later on HMS *India*.

HMS *India* was an armed merchant ship, and an ex-passenger ship. On 8 August 1915 it was on patrol off the Norwegian Coast, attempting to intercept iron ore carriers sailing from Narvik for Germany via Rotterdam. A Swedish vessel, SS *Gloria*, was sighted at 8:30 and HMS *India* intercepted, boarded and searched her. SS *Gloria* was order to sail to Kirkwall. Later that day at 17:40, *U-22* fired a torpedo and though it was sighted, HMS *India* could not avoid the missile, which struck her starboard side. The ship sunk within five minutes.

The attack was approximately two and a half miles off the Norwegian coast and the Norwegian Government complained bitterly to the German Government about this act of war within their waters. Twenty-two officers and 199 ratings were saved, but eleven of the latter died afterwards due to the effects of exposure. Thirty-four-year-old Harold was one of these men. The remaining survivors were interned in Norway.

The *Essex Newsman* reported Harold's death on 28 August 1915:

DROWNED ON THE '*INDIA*'

Seaman Harold George Smith, who was serving on board H.M.S. India when that ship was sunk by a German submarine in neutral waters, was the third son of Mr and Mrs. G A Smith, of Linda Villas, Leigh Road, Hadleigh. He joined the Navy when fifteen years of age and when his period of service expired he was engaged by Hart Accumulator Company, Stratford. The war occurring, he at once rejoined the Navy. He leaves a wife and a little girl, as well as father, mother, five brothers and a sister.

In addition to appearing on the Hadleigh War Memorial, Harold is also commemorated on the Chatham Naval Memorial. He was awarded the 1914-15 Star, Victory and British Medals.

James Anthony Gullett was a signal boy serving on board the battlecruiser HMS *Black Prince* when it was sunk at the Battle of Jutland on 31 May 1916. James was born on 21 April 1899 at Harrow, Middlesex to Frank Baker and Dorcas Emma Gullett. By the time of the 1911 census the family had moved to 8 The Avenue, Kiln Road, in Thundersley.

James Anthony Gullett. (Photograph from the *Southend Standard*)

On the outbreak of war, James' battlecruiser had been following her flagship, *Defence* into action at the first meeting of the two fleets. They were part of the First Cruiser Squadron, deployed as part of a screen force several miles ahead of the main British Fleet. *Defence* was blown up and *Black Prince* for some reason found herself out of touch with the rest of the squadron and the British Fleet. The last recorded communication with the *Black Prince* was a wireless signal received from her at 20:45, reporting a submarine sighting.

Around midnight, in the distance, a line of battleships were spotted by men on board the *Black Prince*. At first they were thought to be British but, as they got closer the captain realised his mistake. He swung his ship round in a desperate effort to escape, but to no avail. Lit up by half a dozen searchlights, the *Black Prince* was raked from stem to stern before she could reply, blowing up with a tremendous explosion and vanishing with all hands. She sank within fifteen minutes; 857 men lost their lives, including seventeen-year-old James Gullett. His body was never recovered and today he is commemorated on the Chatham Memorial.

Frederick Hart was born in 1894 at Lambeth to Richard and Mary Hart. At the time of the 1911 census the family was living at 'Brookland' Kiln Road, Thundersley. Frederick was working on a nearby farm, but in 1912 he joined the navy and during his first three years he served on the *Renown* and the *Edgar*, before transferring to HMS *Queen Mary* as a Stoker First Class.

The *Queen Mary* was the last battleship built by the Royal Navy before the war broke out. Her area of operation was the North Sea within the 1st Battlecruiser Squadron, where her role was to intercept German forces trying to bombard the North Sea coast of England. In so doing she was involved in the Battle of Heligoland Bight in 1914, as part of the Grand Fleet. As she was being refitted in early 1915, she missed the Battle of Dogger Bank, but on 31 May 1916 she was involved in the Battle of Jutland.

During the battle, HMS *Queen Mary* became the target of two German ships, the *Derfflinger* and *Seydlitz*. The following is a report from the HMS *Queen Mary* 1916 Jutland Casualty List:

> *For about five minutes she stood it gallantly. She was fighting splendidly. The Germans say full salvoes were coming from her with fabulous rapidity. Twice already she had been straddled by the Derfflinger, when at 04.26 a plunging salvo crashed upon her deck forward. In a moment there was a dazzling flash of red flame where the salvo fell and then a much heavier explosion rent her amidships.*
>
> *Her bows plunged down and as the Tiger and New Zealand raced by her to port and starboard, her propellers were still revolving high in the air. In another moment, as her two consorts were smothered in a shower of black debris, there was nothing of her left but a dark pillar of smoke rising stem like till it spread hundreds of feet high in the likeness of a vast palm tree.*

The *Queen Mary* lost 1,266 crewmen, including Frederick, with eighteen survivors picked up by destroyers and two by German vessels. In 1991 her wreck was located, resting partly upside down on sand, at a depth of about 60 metres. It has been declared a protected place under the 1986 Protection of Military Remains Act.

Frederick was twenty-three years old when he died and he is commemorated in St Peter's Church, Thundersley and on the Portsmouth Naval Memorial. He was awarded the Victory and British War Medals.

Frederick Potter was born in the parish of Bowers Gifford on 4 July 1896 to William and Martha Potter. He enlisted into the Royal Navy as an able seaman in January 1911 at the tender age of fourteen. He was involved in the first naval battle of the war at Heligoland Bight, on 28 August 1914. Heligoland Bight is the area of sea just off the German coast. The British were keeping a close watch on the German High Seas Fleet stationed there.

The British decided to ambush some of the German destroyers on their regular daily patrols and a fleet of thirty-one destroyers, two cruisers and submarines were dispatched to attack the German destroyers. In the short battle that ensued, the Germans lost three light cruisers and one destroyer, with three more light cruisers damaged, while the British suffered damage to one light cruiser and three destroyers. Germany lost 712 sailors, with 530 more injured and 336 taken prisoner, against thirty-five British sailors killed and forty wounded. The battle was heralded as a resounding victory for the British.

Frederick's next engagement was at the Battle of Dogger Bank. Decoded radio intercepts had given Britain advance warning that a German raiding party was heading towards Dogger Bank, so a British naval force was sent to intercept it. This surprised the smaller slower German fleet and as they returned for home the British chased the fleet and slowly caught up with it, then engaged them with another small victory for the British as a result.

Frederick then moved on to the Cameroons (French Colony, West Central Africa, its coastline lies on the Bight of Bonny, part of the Gulf of Guinea and the Atlantic Ocean) from July 1915 until April 1916, then was with the Lake Tanganyika Expedition between July 1916 and April 1917, when he was transferred to HMS *Salvia* (Q15). Q-ships were also known as Q-boats, decoy vessels, special service ships or mystery ships. They were heavily armed merchant ships with concealed weaponry and the idea was for them to lure submarines into making surface attacks, providing the opportunity for the Q-boat to open fire.

Unfortunately HMS *Salvia* came unstuck, when on 20 June 1917 it was hit by a torpedo from the U-boat *U-94* off the West Coast of Ireland. Frederick was buried at sea. He is commemorated on the Chatham Naval Memorial and the Canvey Island War Memorial.

John Maclure was Chief Steward on board the passenger ship SS *Mesaba*. The *Mesaba* was famous for sending a message at 21.30 pm to the *Titanic,* warning of heavy packed ice. On 1 September 1918, the *Mesaba* was bound for Philadelphia, USA when she was torpedoed by U-Boat *UB-118*, approximately 21 miles from Tuskar Rock, of the south-east coast of County Wexford, Ireland. Twenty lives were lost, with John among the dead.

In command of the German submarine was Kapitänleutnant Hermann Arthur Kraub, who had been lying in wait for easy prey. As soon as he had sighted the *Mesaba* and the ship was in range, he gave the order to attack. One torpedo struck SS *Mesaba* and she immediately began to sink. The submarine had been under the command of Kraub from 22 January until 20 November 1918, when it was surrendered following the cessation of the war and taken under British control. During the time Kraub was in command he sank four ships, *Yturri Bide*, *Ant Cassar*, *City of Glasgow* and lastly SS *Mesaba*.

John was forty-eight years old when he died and left behind a wife, Ada Amelia, who was living at 'Avondale' in Thundersley Road, South Benfleet. He was awarded the Mercantile Marine War Medal and is commemorated on the Tower Hill Memorial, as well as the South Benfleet Memorial.

Arthur James Alden – On the wall of the lych gate entrance to St Mary the Virgin Church in South Benfleet, is a memorial plaque to Arthur Alden and his wife Emily. Arthur was Chief Petty Officer on board HMS *Partridge* when it was sunk on 12 December 1917. His name appears on the Portsmouth Naval Memorial.

On 11 December, HMS *Partridge*, along with HMS *Pellew* and four trawlers, left Lerwick for Bergen with a six merchant ship convoy. HMS *Partridge* was a 'repeat M-class' destroyer, ordered as part of the Emergency War Programme. (Names beginning with 'P' identify the M-class ships).

At around 23:30, off the coast of Norway, south-west of Bjorne Fiord and close to Bergen, the convoy was spotted by four German torpedo boats *G101, G103, G104* and *V100*. At about the same time, the *Partridge*'s crew also sighted the four German boats but, due to a defective searchlight, he was unable to make a challenge for ten minutes. In the meantime the four German torpedo boats were able to get closer and the *Partridge* was hit by shell fire, which shot away the ship's high pressure steam pipes, causing her turbines to stop.

She was then hit by two torpedoes, and the captain gave orders to abandon ship as she sank. She had managed to fire one torpedo, hitting V100 but it failed to explode. All the ships in the convoy were sunk, with the exception of HMS *Pellew*, although it was damaged. *Partridge* lost five officers and ninety-two ratings and a further three officers and twenty-one ratings were picked up by the Germans.

Stanley Gordon King was born on 4 June 1897 and when he enlisted into the Royal Naval Volunteer Reserve on 21 June 1916, he was living at 5 Railway Cottage, South Benfleet, with his mother, Margaret. Before enlisting he was a bioscope operator (a bioscope was an early form of film projector).

He was initially attached to the Royal Naval Division 1st Battalion, then in August he was transferred to the 6th Battalion, then to the 3rd Reserve Battalion at Blandford and for a time he was at the training camp in London, referred to as 'Boarding HMS *Crystal Palace*'. He was drafted for the Mediterranean Expeditionary Force (MEF), before being attached to the Hawke Battalion.

The MEF was the part of the British Army that commanded all Allied forces at Gallipoli and Salonika. The Hawke Battalion had been in Gallipoli since May 1915 and at some stage Stanley must have joined them. The campaign ended on 9 January 1916 and soon afterwards the Battalion was sent to Imbros, a large Greek island, before moving on to the town of Moudros on the Greek island of Lemnos. During the campaign the harbour at Moudros was used as an Allied naval base.

On 18 May 1916, the Hawke Battalion, along with several others, embarked on the troop ship *Franconia* and disembarked at Marseilles on 23 May 1916. The *Franconia* was attacked and sunk by *UB-47* on 4 October 1916, but fortunately there were no troops on board at the time. The 302 survivors were picked up by the hospital ship *Dover Castle*.

The Hawke Battalion became part of an army division and was known as the 63rd (RN) Division. The division moved up to the Somme in October 1916, where they began a period of reconnoitring and extensive training for what was to be their first battle in France, the final large-scale attack of the Battle of the Somme, referred to as the Battle of Ancre.

The battle commenced on 13 November and lasted five days, with a British victory. The Royal Naval Division were decimated during the battle, but they had succeeded where others had failed in previous months. On the first day of the battle, 13 November, Stanley King was killed. Most of those who fell alongside him have no known grave and are commemorated on the Thiepval Memorial. Stanley is buried at the Ancre British Cemetery in Beaumont-Hamel.

He is also commemorated on the South Benfleet War Memorial and he was awarded the 1914-15 Star, Victory and British War Medals. Although not technically killed at sea, he is included here because he was part of the Royal Naval Force.

In *The Times* 'In Memoriam – War' section, on every 13 November the following entry is included:

> *BASTIN – In memory of Capt. E Bastin RMLI and the Officers and men of the Royal Naval Division who gave their lives to take Beaumont Hamel on 13 November 1916.*

Charles Smith was born on 14 November 1881 at South Benfleet, to James and Susan Elizabeth Smith. James is often missing from the censuses, possibly because his occupation was that of a master mariner and therefore he was probably often at sea when the census was taken. Charles decided to follow in his father's footsteps and he signed on initially for twelve years' service with the navy, on 9 November 1900.

It appears that he spent a considerable amount of time at the shore establishment HMS *Pembroke* 11 at Sheerness and at HMS *Vivid* 11, which was an accounting base at Devonport. An an accounting base had a flexible system of allocations, which could mean they were in Chatham, on the river, on shore assignments, or in small vessels, etc. During his time there James seems to have had various roles, before he was promoted to assistant mechanic in January 1912, then senior mechanic a year later.

He joined the fateful HMS *Surprise* on 10 November 1917, only days before it was sunk by a mine. On 23 December 1917, eight destroyers left Harwich to escort a small convoy from the coast of Holland. The rendezvous was off the Maas Light Buoy, a regular meeting point. This was known by the German Navy and they had laid a new minefield in the area in early December.

With visibility reduced by bad weather, the destroyer *Valkyrie* hit a mine about 5 miles west of the light at around 20:00. There seems to have been some confusion after this, with the other destroyer in doubt as to what had happened, but some time later *Torrent* was mined and the *Surprise*, whilst attempting to pick up survivors struck two mines and sank quickly. *Tornado*, another destroyer, manoeuvring in poor visibility to assist, also hit two mines. In total 252 officers and men lost their lives.

Charles is buried at 'S-Gravenzande Cemetery, Holland and he is also commemorated on a grave surround in Great Wakering Cemetery, Essex, as his wife, Elizabeth Jane, was living nearby at the time of his death.

Archibald Arthur Weller's story can only be described as 'murder at sea'. In the early years of the war, the U-boats were a major challenge for the British navy, but after the sinking of the *Lusitania* in 1915, killing 1,201 civilians including ninety-four children and protest from America, the Germans backed down from unconditional submarine warfare. However, as previously noted, they reimplemented unrestricted submarine warfare in March 1917.

The worst subsequent casualty was possibly HMHS *Llandovery Castle*, a Canadian hospital ship en route from Halifax, Nova Scotia to Liverpool, when she was torpedoed off Southern Ireland on 27 June 1918. Although Germany had embarked on unconditional submarine warfare, it was still considered that firing on a hospital ship was against international law and the standing orders of the Germany Navy.

An official report published in 1920 established that on 17 June 1918, the *Llandovery Castle* had arrived at Halifax with 644 military patients. She started her return journey on 20 June 1918, carrying her crew and hospital unit establishment of seven officers, fourteen sisters and seventy-two other ranks. The journey had been uneventful but then, at 21:30, at a distance of 114 miles south-west of the Fastnet Rock, Ireland, she was torpedoed by U-Boat 86. The following explosion wrecked their Marconi radio system, meaning that they could not send an SOS signal. The *Llandovery Castle* sank within approximately ten minutes.

As soon as he realised the seriousness of the situation, the captain of the *Llandovery Castle* ordered the lifeboats to be lowered and it is understood that everyone on board, other than those already killed by the explosion, managed to get off the ship. However, only twenty-four survived in one lifeboat, and only six of the hospital personnel: Major T. Lyon, Sergeant A. Knight, Private F. W. Cooper, Private G. R. Hickman, Private S. A. Taylor and Private W. Pilot, all belonging to the Canadian Army Medical Corps.

What followed the sinking of the *Llandovery Castle* was the U-boat captain's attempt to destroy the lifeboats and their occupants, in order to conceal all evidence of the fact that he had sunk a clearly identifiable hospital ship. He not only tried to run down the lifeboats but also opened fire on those survivors still in the water. At one point the submarine pulled alongside the lifeboat that Major T. Lyon was in and he was roughly dragged on board, where he was accused of being an American flying officer, among another seven American officers on board. Obviously the major denied that this was the case and asserted that the *Llandovery Castle* was a hospital ship and had not carried any ammunition. He was eventually placed back into the lifeboat, while others were taken on board the submarine and questioned. Once they got the lifeboat away from the submarine it attempted to run them down, only missing by a couple of feet.

Major Lyon commented in his report about the sinking of the *Llandovery Castle*: 'I can emphatically state, that the submarine made no attempt to rescue any one but on the contrary did everything in its power to destroy every trace of the ship and its personnel and crew.'

Remaining survivors found themselves being sucked down and drowned as the *Llandovery Castle* sank. Sergeant A. Knight found himself in command of a lifeboat with fourteen nurses. In his statement he said:

> *I estimate we were together in the boat about eight minutes. In that whole time I did not hear a complaint or murmur from one of the sisters. There was not a cry for help or any outward evidence of fear. In the entire time I overheard only one remark when the matron, Nursing Sister M. M. Fraser, turned to me as we drifted helplessly towards the stern of the ship and asked:- 'Sergeant, do you think there is any hope for us?'*
>
> *I replied, 'No' seeing for myself our helplessness without oars and the sinking condition of the stern of the ship.*
>
> *A few seconds later we were drawn into the whirlpool of the submerged afterdeck and the last I saw of the nursing sisters was as they were thrown over the side of the boat. All were wearing life-belts and of the fourteen two were in nightdress, the others in uniform.*

Sergeant Knight concluded that it was doubtful if any of the survivors came to the surface again, although he himself sank and came up three times, before he finally managed to cling to a piece of wreckage and be picked up by Major Lyon's boat. The nurses beside him had volunteered for Front Line service and for many months they would have endured the terrible conditions on the Western Front, treating enemy wounded as well as Allied troops.

The twenty-four people in the only surviving lifeboat were eventually rescued by HMS *Lysander*. HMS *Morea* later steamed through the wreckage and its Captain, Kenneth Cummins, recalled the horror:

> *We were in the Bristol Channel, quite well out to sea and suddenly we began going through corpses. The Germans had sunk a British hospital ship, the Llandovery Castle and we were sailing through floating bodies. We were not allowed to stop – we just had to go straight through. It was quite horrific and my reaction was to vomit over the edge. It was something we could never have imagined... particularly the nurses: seeing these bodies of women and nurses, floating in the ocean, having been there some time. Huge aprons and skirts in billows, which looked almost like sails because they dried in the hot sun.*

In total, 234 lives were lost and among them was Archibald Weller, a First Bed Steward in the Mercantile Marine Regiment. He was twenty-four years of age at the time and the son of Arthur and Rhoda Weller of 'Ryecroft', South View Road, South Benfleet. Archibald was posthumously awarded the Mercantile Marine War Medal and is commemorated on the Tower Hill Memorial, London and the South Benfleet War Memorial.

After the war, the captain of *U-86*, Lieutenant Helmet Patzig and two of his lieutenants, Ludwig Dithmar and John Bolt were accused of war crimes. Patzig left Germany and avoided extradition, but the other two were convicted and sentenced to four years in prison, from which they escaped. At a court of appeal they were later acquitted on the grounds that the captain was solely responsible.

Ernest John Barttram was born on Canvey Island on 28 May 1894 to John and Elizabeth Barttram. He joined the Royal Navy in

September 1917, as an able seaman and was serving on HMS *Kilkeel*, a patrol gunboat, when he died of pneumonia on 6 February 1919 at Longhope, Scotland. He may have been among the thousands of servicemen who survived the war only to die of the Spanish flu, which had been raging throughout Europe since 1918.

The *Kilkeel* was commissioned in August 1918 and never saw active service. Whether Ernest served on any other previous ships is unknown. He is buried along with his brother Bertie, who had died a year earlier in St Katherine's Churchyard on Canvey Island and is commemorated on the Canvey Island War Memorial.

'Ye Mariners of Deutschland: A Naval Ode'

Ye mariners of Deutschland,
Who guard your Baltic Seas,
Whose flag has waved some dozen years
In harbour and at ease,
Your Kaiser's standard furl again,
To fight your own fleet go,
And creep through the deep
When the tempests do not blow,
When the British fleet is far away,
And the stormy winds don't blow!

The spirits of your brothers
Shall start from every wave,
For you shot them down on their own decks,
The ocean was their grave,
Where they, your murdered brothers, fell.
What shame your hearts shall show
As you creep through the deep
When tempest do not blow,
When the British fleet is out of sight,
And the stormy winds don't blow!

Germania loves a bulwark
Well fortified with steel;
Her fleet feels safe at Heligoland,
And quite secure at Kiel.
With pistol shots her officers

Quell their own men, not the foe,
As they roar for the shore
When the stormy tempest blow,
When the tempest rages loud and long,
And they fain would go below!
The meteor flag of England
Shall yet terrific burn,
Till the Prussians' troubled night depart,
And the star of peace return.
Then, then, ye harbour-sailors!
Our song and feast shall flow
To the shame of your name.
Who laid your own men low.
In murderous fight, that summer night,
When the tempest did blow.
(Author unknown, published in the
Chelmsford Chronicle, 25 September 1914.)

Approximately 3,200 merchant and fishing vessels were lost during the First World War, along with the lives of nearly 15,000 Merchant Seamen. Added to this was the loss of around 150 Royal Navy ships, with approximately 35,000 lives, and those like Stanley King who transferred to Infantry Units, such as the Hawke Battalion.

CHAPTER 5

War in the Air

The First World War not only involved many countries but also saw entirely new methods of warfare, including mining, tanks, the use of gas, submarines, aeroplanes and aerial bombing.

For centuries, following the attempt by the Spanish Armada in 1588, Britain had appeared reasonably safe from invasion because of the natural barrier provided by the English Channel. The last serious invasion attempt had been made by Napoleon in 1805, when his fleet was defeated by Nelson in the Battle of Trafalgar. So the shock was palpable when, on 19 January 1915, two Zeppelin airships, dropped twenty-four 50 kg high explosive bombs on Great Yarmouth, Sheringham, Kings Lynn and surrounding villages. Four people were killed and sixteen were injured, with the damage from the bombings estimated at £7,740.

The Zeppelin was a type of rigid airship developed by the German Count Ferdinard von Zeppelin in the early twentieth century. His ideas had been formulated in the latter part of the nineteenth century and were patented in Germany in 1895 and America in 1899. Zeppelins were first flown commercially in 1910 and by mid-1914 they had carried over 34,000 passengers on over 1,500 flights.

It was not long before the German Army and Navy took an interest in Zeppelins, perceiving a great advantage to using them in reconnaissance missions. The German Navy had commissioned fifteen Zeppelins by 1915 and mainly used them for patrols over the North Sea and Baltic. However, soon the German High Command spotted the possibilities of carrying out aerial bombing raids, as the Zeppelins

OUT FOR VICTORY.

THE AIRMAN.
Who means to teach the Hun a lesson.

'Out for Victory'.
(Cartoon postcard)

were considerably more capable than the current range of light fixed-wing aeroplanes. They could carry a greater bomb load, in addition to multiple machine guns, and had a greater range.

Weather foiled any further Zeppelin attacks on Britain until 29 April, when Zeppelin LZ.38, commanded by Erich Linnarz raided Ipswich, and then on 10 May he also attacked Southend. One of the incendiary bombs that he dropped fell a few yards from the moored prison ship RMS *Royal Edward*. The first internees had arrived in Southend on 18 November 1914, and were likely to have been mainly German nationals who were living in Britain on the outbreak of war. The internees were able to pay for beds in any of the first, second and third class cabins, which were rented out at between 2 and 5 shillings a week, depending on how many were sharing a cabin.

On one occasion the American Embassy in Berlin sent over a diplomat to inspect the treatment and conditions of the prisoners. *Royal Edward*, being a passenger ship, could accommodate over 1,000 passengers. At night, for security reasons, the prisoners were locked in below deck. This was quite a frightening experience for them, as they knew that Zeppelins could come at any time and a direct hit would mean certain death.

There were two other prison ships moored nearby off Southend Pier, SS *Ivernia* and RMS *Saxonia*. Due to the expense of hiring ships for such purpose, it was agreed that ships would cease to be used by the middle of April. However, the three at Southend were kept there until early June. The *Essex Newsman* reported on 5 June 1915 that about 500 civilian prisoners had recently been removed from the internment ships lying off the pier to an inland internment camp.

On 10 May, Erich Linnarz dropped several bombs over Southend, fortunately missing the internment ships, and travelled up the Thames

HMS Ivernia. (Postcard)

as far as Canvey. Fierce anti-aircraft fire from a battery at Cliffe on the Kentish coast forced him to turn back, and he dropped his remaining bombs on Southend. He also appears to have dropped a message which was found the following day on Canvey Island. It read: 'You English! We have come and we will come again soon – kill or cure – German.'

An eyewitness report of the bombing appeared in the *Southend Standard*:

> *About three o'clock I was aroused from my sleep by the sound of an explosion. I got up, put my head out of the window and heard the noise of an engine. I woke my brother up and we went downstairs and stood in the roadway. My brother saw the Zeppelin overhead and it was at a great height.*

Linnarz was true to his word, he was back again on 17 May, when he attacked Dover and Ramsgate, before returning to bomb Southend

Linnarz and the crew of LZ 38. (Photograph reproduced with permission of the Canvey Island Archive website)

on 31 May. These four attacks resulted in seven civilians killed, 35 injured and seven properties destroyed.

The raids continued throughout the summer of 1915 and the Zeppelins were given the name of 'Baby Killers'. The fact that they appeared to be able to pass through the British air defences with such ease led the government to implement strong press restrictions on the reporting of air raids. Following these attacks, Hadleigh Parish Council allocated £75 for the purchase of fire-fighting equipment, including a handcart, scaling ladders, a hose and canvas buckets. This led to the formation of a special volunteer fire brigade.

On 31 March 1916 the British tasted their first victory during the Zeppelin raids,when L15 flew up the Thames as far as Rainham, where, heavy gunfire caused the commander, Lieutenant Breithaupt, to turn north into Essex and drop his bombs. Flying alongside him, Second Lieutenant Ridley hit the Zeppelin with twenty rounds, but no sooner had L15 escaped Ridley when it was attacked by another BE 2c from Hainault Farm. Escaping again, it was eventually hit by a shell from a battery at Tank Hill Purfleet, commanded by Captain John Harris. This forced L 15 into the Thames estuary. The trawler *Olivine* saved all of the crew of the L 15, except the signaller, Albrecht, who stayed behind to try to destroy the Zeppelin and was apparently killed. The whole incident was clearly seen from the coast of Southend and Canvey Island.

British air defences slowly improved and by mid-1916, there were 271 anti-aircraft guns (one of these gun battery placements was at Deadmans Point, on Canvey Island) and 258 searchlights. Along with the development of incendiary bullets, this gave British aircraft a better chance of success against the German airships, as was seen with the destruction of LZ 32, which crashed at Great Burstead. They were, however, still a threat throughout the war.

The last air raid on Britain was played out over East Anglia on 5 August 1918. When crossing the North Sea at around 16,000 feet and heading towards the coast of Norfolk, five Zeppelins appeared, flying in a V-formation. It was the first attack in four months and probably very unexpected, as it was becoming obvious that Britain and the Allies were winning the war. On board LZ 70, which was some 693 feet in length, was the leader of the airships Fregattenkapitän Peter Strasser, the Chief Commander of German Imperial Navy Zeppelins. As LZ 70

LZ 32 crash site at Great Burstead. (Postcard)

approached the English coast, pilot Major Edgar Cadbury and gunner Captain Robert Leckie were waiting at Denes Air Station at Great Yarmouth, in their two seater De Havilland DH4. They were quickly in the air and dusk had just fallen when they reached the required height, approaching LZ 70 more or less head on.

Captain Leckie fired a long burst of explosive bullets from his Lewis machine gun at 600 yards, blowing a large hole in LZ 70 fuselage and setting it on fire. After it plunged into the sea, killing all the crew, the remaining four Zeppelins immediately abandoned the operation and returned to their home base. This marked the end of the Zeppelin war, which had by now seen the deaths of 2,000 Zeppelin crew and 550 civilians.

The History of Military Flight

Military flight originally started with the French invention of the balloon, which was used for observation as early as the French Revolution. Britain lagged behind and was slow to adopt this new innovation, and it was not until 1878 that the first Army Balloon School was established at Woolwich. It was followed four years later by a factory and training school established at Chatham as a unit of the Royal Engineers, which was named the 'Balloon Factory'. The Balloon Factory was soon moved to Farnborough, Hampshire and thus, in the infancy of British aviation, an association began which, through time and various name changes, eventually became the Royal Air Force.

Balloons with tail fins, known as Kite Balloons, saw service in both World Wars, in both defence and observation mode. The airship was to follow but again Britain was slow to copy this new German technology, and the first British airship was not completed until 1907. More airships and balloons were built at Farnborough, although the new type of flying machine, the aeroplane, gradually overshadowed them.

Again Britain was far behind both the French and the Germans in developing the flying machine and it was not until 1911 that the War Office started to take the new invention seriously and the old Balloon Section was expanded into an Air Battalion. The naval armaments race worried British politicians and, probably because of this, they did not give sufficient thought to air power. Germany was continuing to develop an impressive airship fleet, while the British government found that by the end of 1911 it had very few serviceable aircraft; it was thought that there were only eleven flying men in the British Army and only eight in the Royal Navy.

However, the Royal Navy had already built its first seaplane, as it was gravely concerned with the possible threat from submarines and by 1914 there were 16 seaplanes in service, fitted with transmitters, while five coastal air stations had transmitters and receivers. In the meantime the Royal Flying Corps was established on 13 March 1912 and it included a Military Wing, a Naval Wing, a Central Flying School, a Reserve and the Royal Aircraft Factory at Farnborough to provide aircraft for both wings.

The idea was that the two wings would work closely together, but in fact the opposite happened and they drifted further apart. The army concentrated on reconnaissance, getting accurate information for the troops on the ground, yet on the other hand, the Navy Wing began to consider using aircraft in an offensive mode. As war approached the differences between them grew greater and in July 1914 the Naval Wing became known as the Royal Naval Air Service (RNAS). Slowly, with practical experiment and some good luck, the primitive aircraft were fitted with limited navigation tools, armaments, such as machine guns and very basic bomb sights.

On the outbreak of war, the Royal Flying Corps (RFC) went to France to support the British Expeditionary Force with just sixty-three aeroplanes, 105 officers and ninety-five motor transport vehicles. The RNAS stayed in Britain to defend the Home Front and shipping against attack by hostile aircraft. Although the aircraft proved extremely valuable in obtaining information through reconnaissance in all weathers, and even in dangerous situations it was the fighter aircraft that were to dominate air operations after the first year of the war. As the war progressed, improvements continued to be made, but it was becoming a strain for the authorities to work with two separate wings and eventually, after months of political debate, the two wings were combined to form the Royal Air Force on 1 April 1918.

Air combat, however, was very primitive at first and because of this it was extremely rare for pilots to do more than to conduct reconnaissance by air. There were some early bombing raids, although the 1914 aircraft could only carry very small loads and the bombing was very inaccurate. Air combat started with a few grenades and various objects, such as grappling hooks, being thrown out of the aircraft. Pilots eventually progressed to firing hand-held firearms, but pistols were too inaccurate at this range and the single shot rifles were unlikely to score a hit. In October 1914 a French pilot opened fire on a German aircraft with a machine gun for the first time and the era of air combat began, as aircraft were fitted with machine guns.

North Benfleet Airfield

The London Air Defence Area (LADA) established a number of airfields around the capital in 1915, with the specific aim of defending against the growing threat of enemy airships. Hainault Farm, later renamed RAF Fairlop, and Suttons Farm, later dubbed RAF Hornchurch, were added to the existing airfields in Essex of North

Crashed aircraft. (Cartoon postcard)

Weald and Rochford to cover the eastern approaches to London. By early 1916 it was considered necessary to increase the number of airfields required at least for emergency landings. With this in mind the authorities decided to close the gap of some 21 miles between Rochford and Suttons Farm.

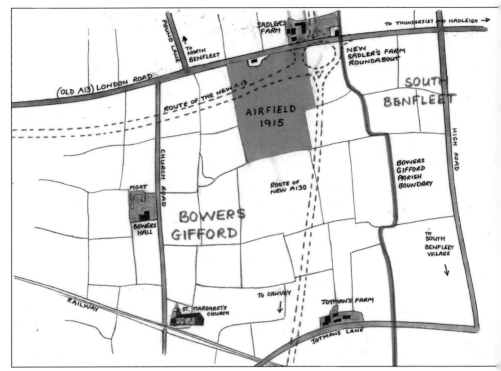

Map of the airfield at Bowers Gifford. The landing site was very close to the Sadlers Farm roundabout and the new A13 and A130 road, which heads south to Canvey Island. Although the site was within the boundaries of Bowers Gifford it was referred to as 'North Benfleet'. (Drawing by Sue Ranford)

A permanent night landing ground was proposed in the Pitsea area. The initial area chosen adjacent to the River Thames was low-lying and marshy, therefore liable to flooding. However, further inland the higher ground was more suitable and a site was selected comprised of three arable fields in the Parish of Bowers Gifford, two owned by Charles Bayley at Sadlers Farm and one belonging to James Buckenham at Jotmans Farm. The fields are just outside the parish of South Benfleet.

The site became operational in April 1916 and was categorised a Second Class site To be used for emergency landings. It had a windsock and wet weather shelter for the personnel manning the site, along with ground arrow signals. In September 1916, the landing ground was allocated to No. 7 (HD) Squadron, part of 'A' Flight based at Rochford and in August 1917 it was also allocated to No.61 (HD) Squadron from Rochford.

The only recorded instance of the site receiving an emergency occurred on the night of 30 September 1917, when 37 Home Defence sorties were flown against eleven Gothas raiding London. Sutton Farm No. 78 (HD) Squadron sent up five of its Sopwith 1 ½ Strutters on patrol, of which B2593, crewed by Lieutenant J.S. Castle and Airman First Class H, Daws, suffered engine problems and made a precautionary landing at Sadlers Farm. The *Daily Mail* reported on the following day that eleven people had been killed and eighty-two injured in the raid.

Other squadrons were allocated to the landing ground, but very little use was made of it and in March 1919 the Air Ministry returned the land to its owners to allow farming to continue. However, in May 1936 Sadlers Farm hosted the British Air Display, which included such aircraft as the Avro 504, DH Fox Moth, and Hawker Tomtit.

South-East Essex Pilots in the Great War:
Henry Arthur Carey was born in Thundersley on 19 March 1888 to George and Sarah Carey. At some point he joined the RAF and took part in the Battle of Loos, where he was awarded the Distinguished Conduct Medal. The citation read:

> *For distinguished conduct in the field at Loos, 27 September 1915. He went out and reconnoitred the enemy's wire by himself, after which he returned and piloted the bombing party to their appointed place, being slightly wounded in doing so. He then went back and guided the remainder of the party under rifle and machine gun fire, being a second and third time slightly wounded. Finally he remained in action with his party until ordered to retire. He set a fine example of courage and devotion to duty.*

Henry survived the war and returned home to marry Daisy Alderton on 8 May 1919.

Reginald Cuthbert Whiteside was born on 19 July 1896 and he enlisted into the Royal Navy Volunteer Reserve on 21 September 1915.

He was living at the time with his parents, the Rev. W.C. Whiteside and Laura Whiteside, at 'Longlands' in South Benfleet. It would appear that he was immediately appointed Temporary Sub-Lieutenant.

At the outset of war there was a surplus of nearly 30,000 men in the Royal Navy who could not be allocated roles on any ship of war. It was recognised that at least two Naval Brigades and a Brigade of Marines could be formed from the reserves for operations on land, alongside the army infantry divisions.

Reginald appears to have drifted back and forth between the 3rd Battalion and the 2nd Battalion, before settling down with the 5th Battalion. The battalions were named after famous naval heroes, the 2nd was named 'Hawke', the 3rd 'Benbow' and the 5th 'Nelson'. After spending the first nine months of his war service in England, he arrived at the British Base Camp in Etaples on 8 July 1916. Etaples was an old fishing town and port on the mouth of the River Canche in the region of Pas de Calais. It became the largest military camp that Britain ever set up overseas, at times housing 100,000 personnel.

The Battle of the Somme had commenced a few days earlier, on 1 July, and it was to dominate the rest of the year, until it finally came to an end in November. It is likely that Reginald saw plenty of action with the Nelson Battalion, but on 27 October 1916 he was transferred to the Royal Flying Corps (RFC) as an observer on probation, joining 18 Squadron.

On the afternoon of 20 December 1916, Reginald and his pilot, Second Lieutenant Lionel George D'Arcy, were flying their De Havilland FE2b in the sky over Moreuil, Northern France when they encountered the famous Red Baron, who was flying his Albatros D11 No 491/16.

The Red Baron fired first, damaging the engine of the FE2b and it is believed that Reginald was wounded during this attack. As the British aircraft began to fall from the sky, the Red Baron followed his initial shots with more bursts of fire. The aircraft crashed, killing both men. It was the Red Baron's fourteenth 'kill'. Both airmen may have been buried by the German military, as was the custom, since their bodies have never been found. They are commemorated on the Arras Flying Service Memorial in France and the South Benfleet War Memorial.

At the time of his death Reginald's parents were living in Auckland, New Zealand. Reginald was posthumously awarded the Victory and British War Medals.

Manfred Albrecht Freiberr von Richthofen (known as the 'Red Baron') was considered the top flying ace of the war, with 80 air combat victories to his name. He was born on 2 May 1892 in Kleinburg near Breslau, Germany, into a prominent Prussian aristocratic family. His father was Major Albrecht P.K.J. Freiberr von Richthofen (Freiberr was often translated as 'Baron').

When the war started, Manfred served as a cavalry reconnaissance officer on both the Eastern and Western fronts, but it was soon realised that with the development of trench warfare, cavalry operations were becoming outdated and his regiment was disbanded. Bored by his subsequent role, he applied to the Imperial Germany Army Air Service. It is understood that he wrote in his application: 'I have not gone to war in order to collect cheese and eggs but for another purpose.'

He was accepted and transferred to the flying service in May 1915 as an observer and even in this role he is said to have shot down a French aircraft, but as it fell behind Allied lines it could not be confirmed. In October 1915 he entered training as a pilot. By January 1917, after his sixteenth confirmed kill, he received the Pour le Mérite (informally known as the 'Blue Max'), the highest military honour in Germany at the time. He gained command of a fighter squadron and took the rather flamboyant step of having his aircraft painted red – hence his nickname.

On 6 July 1917 he received a head wound during combat, but after a period of convalescence he returned to the skies. Then, at 11.00am on 21 April 1918 he received a fatal wound as he was flying over Morlancourt Ridge, near the Somme River. At the time, the Baron was pursuing at low altitude a novice Canadian pilot, Lieutenant May, but he was spotted by another Canadian, Captain Brown, who dived steeply to intervene. The Baron turned to avoid the attack and continued his pursuit of May. At some point he was hit by a single bullet and he barely managed to land his aircraft before he died. The question of whether he was shot down by Brown or by ground fire remains.

In common with most Allied air officers, Major Blake, who was responsible for von Richthofen's remains, regarded him with great respect and organised a full military funeral. Von Richthofen was buried in the cemetery at the village of Bertangles, near Amiens, on 22 April 1918.

Percy Louis Smith was born in 1895 at Ramsden Crays, Essex, the eldest son of Frederick and Mary Ann Smith. By 1901 the family were living in Hadleigh and before enlisting Percy was employed as a cycle repairer for seven years. He initially joined the Essex Regiment in 1914, then served with the Royal Engineers and the Bedfordshire Regiment, before being posted to the Royal Flying Corps 111th Squadron, at the rank of Airman Second Class. After a short spell of leave, he was sent to Egypt in early 1915. He was part of a group of men repairing an aero engine when they were hit by a bomb dropped from enemy aircraft. Percy died two days later on 3 December 1917 at Gaza Military Hospital and was buried in the Gaza War Cemetery. He is commemorated on the Hadleigh War Memorial.

Reginald Whiteside and Percy Smith are the only two First World War servicemen from the four south-east Essex parishes who eventually ended up in one of the Flying Corps. This is not surprising, as aerial warfare did not play as fundamental a role in the First World War as in the Second. In this conflict bombing was used more as a psychological weapon than a practical one. However, the war did encourage the rapid improvement in the development of the aeroplane and produced a new generation of pilots and aircraft designers, whose work would bear fruit when the Second World War broke out twenty years later.

CHAPTER 6

The Land War

Asleep they lie – son – husband – father – lover,
At home, in France, or farther overseas
The earth enfolds them, and the grasses cover,
Who live in proud and loving memories.

One by the Menin Road, may be, is lying,
One where the Somme's bird-haunted rushes wave,
O'er one the uncooled desert wind is sighing
One has the deep sea for his silent grave
                    (Lieutenant-Colonel F.W.D Bendall)

There is no doubt that the various battles at sea and in the air played a massive part in the final outcome of the First World War. The Royal Navy ensured that Germany never controlled the high seas. The Royal Flying Corps was transformed from its position in the early days of the war as a fleet of unarmed, slow, observation machines, into an effective fighting machine under the newly founded Royal Air Force.

However, in most narratives of the First World War it is the land war that takes precedence. The trench warfare on the Western Front, the use of gas, the retreat at Mons, the terrible losses during the battles of Gallipoli, the Somme, Ypres etc. and foremost the unbelievable heavy numbers of casualties. On the outbreak of hostilities, Britain's land army was very small compared with the German, French and Russian forces, consisting of just over 100,000 men in early August 1914. Yet, with the recruitment drive for volunteers and forces from

Britain's Empire coming to its aid, Britain soon started to catch up. Nevertheless, new recruits would constantly be needed, right up to the end of the war, because of the high casualty rate. Germany had miscalculated the amount of help that Britain could expect from its Empire, having assumed that many of the countries then under British control would take the opportunity to demand independence. Nothing could have been further from the truth, as people from all parts of the British Empire rallied to the defence of the 'Mother Country'.

Canada led the way, followed by Australia, New Zealand, India, South Africa, Nigeria, the West Indies – even Zulu and Basuto tribesmen came forward, along with those from tiny Pacific Islands. Soon these colonial troops also began to sustain casualties. The first Bermudian serviceman to be killed was 22-year-old Officers' Cook First Class William Edmund Smith, who had joined the Royal Navy and was drowned when HMS *Aboukir* was torpedoed on 22 September 1914.

Not only men were sent to Britain's aid by these countries but also supplies. For example, in Canada, Alberta offered half a million bushels of oats and civil servants offered a percentage of their wages; British Columbia gave 25,000 cases of tinned salmon; Manitoba 50,000 bags of flour; New Brunswick 100,000 bushels of potatoes; and Nova Scotia 100,000 tons of coal; Montreal gave £30,000; Quebec sent 4,000,000 lbs of cheese; and Saskatchewan provided 1,500 horses.

Confidence was bolstered by all this overseas assistance, but the British military authorities soon encountered an unexpected problem at home. Inundated by volunteers, the military was unable to provide basic training quickly enough and many new recruits found themselves in cold, damp tents or billeted in local pubs, often without proper uniforms or weapons. What followed would – at least early on in the war – have been two months of very basic and rough training, before troops were shipped overseas. This meant that in many cases soldiers found themselves at the Front woefully under-prepared to fight and face the privations of trench warfare.

The first thing that most soldiers learned in the trenches was to keep their heads below the parapet at all times, to avoid providing a target for enemy snipers. The environment too caused fresh recruits problems, as they had to cope with, at times, being waist-deep in water or wading about with mud up to their knees. The trenches were breeding grounds for diseases and infectious skin complaints, as well as flesh-rotting

British Sentry in Flanders. (Postcard)

trench foot which could induce gangrene. During the winter months with snow, ice and sub-zero temperatures, soldiers were at high risk of frostbite and hypothermia. Year round troops were also plagued by lice and rats in their thousands.

Then, of course, there was the problem of performing basic bodily functions. Many of the soldiers would have come from households where a toilet was little more than a cesspit in a shed at the bottom of the garden, perhaps shared with several other families, but at least this would have been emptied out on a regular basis. In the trenches, the latrines usually consisted of deep holes, with a hole cut into the board placed across it for a seat.

The soldiers' diet was very monotonous, and at best they would have received corned beef (bully beef), bacon and sausages, rissoles, hard biscuits, tinned pork fat and beans, bread and jam. Although their diet was still a lot better than that of the poorest families back home, many eagerly awaited parcels of food from friends and family. Early on in the war cooked food was carried into the trenches from the rear and transported along the communication trenches, but often delays occurred and soldiers had to improvise.

During a break in an offensive, the daily routine for soldiers usually began with a period of 'stand to', in which the men would make ready for an enemy attack. This normally lasted for one and half hours, then if there was no action the men would 'stand down' for breakfast. The rest of the day would be divided into weapons inspections, sentry duties and many other various tasks, such as trench and communication repairs. Just before dusk there would be another period of 'stand to', with the soldiers then rotating on sentry duty throughout the night.

Signalling stand down. (Illustration from *The War Illustrated*)

'Break of Day in the Trenches'

The darkness crumbles away.
It is the same old druid time as ever.
Only a live thing leaps my hand,
A queer sardonic rat,
As I pull the parapet's poppy
To stick behind my ear.
Droll rat, they would shoot you if they knew
Your cosmopolitan sympathies.
Now you have touched this English hand
You will do the same to a German
Soon, no doubt, if it be your pleasure
To cross the sleeping green between.
It seems you inwardly grin as you pass
Strong eyes, fine limbs, haughty athletes,
less chanced than you for life,
Bonds to the whims of murder,
Sprawled in the bowels of the earth,
The torn fields of France.
What do you see in our eyes
At the shrieking iron and flame
Hurled through still heavens?
What quaver – what heart aghast?
Poppies whose roots are in men's veins
Drop and are ever dropping:
But mine in my ear is safe,
Just a little white with the dust.
(By Isaac Rosenberg, Died 1 April 1918)

The British Tommy would spend roughly four to eight days on the Front Line, before being pulled back into support or reserve positions. This meant that soldiers could still be within shelling distance of enemy heavy artillery. For a real rest, troops would be pulled further back and housed in all sorts of billets, from tents to wooden huts or, if they were lucky, they might be billeted with local civilians, often sleeping in farmhouses or converted public buildings. Life behind the line was still very hard and discipline strict. There were few luxuries other than a decent night's sleep, but if troops were fortunate enough to be billeted near a village or town they could do a little shopping, go to local bars or even enjoy a bit of sightseeing.

Punishment for any infractions was very harsh and most British soldiers lived under the threat of court martial. Non-Commissioned Officers (NCOs) dealt with most of the offences committed by troops, some of which could be very trivial, such as failure to perform a minor order. The most common punishments were being confined to barracks, pay deductions, loss of leave or rest periods, or additional fatigue duties. More extreme measures included Field Punishment No.1, during which the convicted man was handcuffed to a fixed object, often a gun wheel, for up to 21 days, for several hours a day, through all weathers. This punishment was instituted on 60,210 occasions during the First World War. A total of 3,080 death sentences were handed out to British troops, but only 346 men were shot, as the majority had their sentences commuted to a term of imprisonment.

Perhaps surprisingly, given the constant reports of casualties, major battles happened on a relatively infrequent basis during the Great War, and a soldier would only rarely be involved in a major offensive, a harrowing and unforgettable experience which many could only describe as hell on earth. Thousands of soldiers never participated directly in a major battle, yet there were plenty of skirmishes in between, ranging from artillery fire through to the violent experience of trench raids, which were undertaken by both sides with the intention of taking prisoners or destroying enemy positions. Trench raids came in all shapes and sizes – perhaps just a commander and a few men on a special mission, or an entire company or battalion making a daylight assault with artillery support across No-Man's Land. If the raiding party reached the enemy's trench, then brutal hand-to-hand fighting took place.

The following letter from Private H.J. Parker of the 2nd Essex Regiment (Pompadours) helps to give an insight into daily life in the trenches:

We were caught unexpectedly while trench-digging. It was thought the French cavalry were in front of us but it proved to be the Germans. In my part of the trench four of us were trying to escape. The next chap to me but one had the top of his head blown off. This was the first case of the kind I had seen but heaven only knows I have seen scores since. Well, I thought the best thing to do was to lie in the trench for a while.

The Germans came along, took my rifle and broke it up. Then they made me lie down in the firing line. I was not the only one captured; there were lots from different regiments. Thank God I got out of it all right, for our artillery got into action and the firing was too much for them. We then commenced our retirement, which lasted fourteen days and nights. Then we were reinforced and commenced a general advance.

We have just left some trenches where there has been a big battle. We took these trenches at night time. The dead were lying in front of us like stones. We are about 400 yards from the enemy's trenches and we have to keep our heads down, or we would soon get popped over by snipers. One company of ours had about ninety six casualties the other day.

(*Essex Newsman*, 7 November 1914.)

Another view comes from a letter reported in the *Chelmsford Chronicle* three years later, in November 1917, from Private Thomas Stanley Pannell of the Artists' Rifles, who was writing home from Cardiff Hospital:

As this the first time I have been allowed up since I got hit, you will know that I have not much seen of this city yet. My usual luck attended me when I went over the top, or I should not be here now. It was a grand sight to see our chaps go over and those who got through put the wind up Fritz with the bayonet. Our battalion advanced up to their waist in mud.

All I have got is a fractured shoulder and two places in the back, caused by shrapnel. One is two inches from the spine, so I was very lucky. They operated on me as soon as I reached the casualty clearing station, which is about twenty miles behind the line. But I walked all the way from where I was hit to a first aid post, a mile walk. If I hadn't done so, I should have most likely gone the same way as some of my pals did.

In hindsight it seems amazing that so many volunteered, even after reports were flooding in of the horrors they would face at the Front. The following pages include some of the personal stories of the brave men from the four south-east Essex parishes, who went to war for adventure and for the salvation of the British Isles, along with details of the conflicts they were involved in.

Canvey Island Soldiers in the Great War:
Raymond John Machin was born in 1898 at East Woodhay, Hampshire. By 1911 he was living with his family at the School House on Canvey Island, where his father George was the schoolmaster. Raymond enlisted into the Duke of Wellington's (West Riding Regiment) and on 21 September 1918 the *Essex Newsman* reported that: 'Second Lieutenant R. J. Machin, eldest son of the headmaster of Canvey Island Church School, has been awarded the Military Cross for great determination and good leadership while wounded.'

Then, on 7 November 1918, the *London Gazette* reports further details of the award: 'His Majesty the King has been graciously pleased to approve of the award in recognition of his gallantry and devotion to duty in the field.' The *Gazette* report continued:

> *Temporary Second Lieutenant Raymond John Machin, West Riding Regiment, for conspicuous gallantry and devotion to duty. He took command of the company when the commander was wounded and led them forward. In spite of a painful wound he brought them to the objective and consolidated, remaining at his post for twenty-four hours until ordered to the dressing station. His example of courage and endurance greatly inspired his men.*

It has not be possible to establish the various offensives in which Raymond Machin was involved, other than to note that his regiment was in the thick of the fighting from the beginning to the end of the war. The regiment raised twenty-three battalions, was awarded sixty-three battle honours and five Victoria Crosses, and lost 7,870 men in the course of the war.

Raymond was among those who survived, in fact he had returned home by the time the 1918 electoral register was produced, probably

British Tommies going over the top. (Postcard)

demobbed early because of his injury. He died in 1958 in Surrey at the age of sixty and, in addition to his Military Cross, he was awarded the Victory and British War Medals.

Raymond's younger brother, **Frederick Ronald Machin**, also volunteered on 1 October 1918, just over a month before the end of the war. He enlisted into the 3rd-13th London Regiment, at the rank of private. As he was then aged under nineteen, he spent a year training in England and was later transferred to the army reserve on 27 January 1919, before finally being discharged on 31 March 1920. On 20 July 1921 he re-enlisted at Southend into the 6th Battalion Essex Regiment Defence Force, at the rank of private, but again it does not appear that he was posted overseas and a year later he was discharged.

Edward Ernest Depper's origins remain a mystery, although he may have been a Canvey lad when he went to war, as he enlisted into the 7th Rifle Brigade (The Prince Consort's Own). His rank was that of Corporal, then he was later promoted to Sergeant. His regiment was mobilised for war and landed at Boulogne on 20 May 1915. The 7th Rifle Brigade became engaged in various actions on the Western Front during 1915, including the German Gas attack at Chateau and Hooge, a small village located near Ypres, in Belgium. Chateau had been captured by the British, after the detonation of an underground mine on 19 July 1915, forming a crater 6 metres deep by 40 metres wide.

The Germans retaliated on 30 July, this time in addition to gas (which could be neutralised to an extent with gas masks), with jets of burning fuel. German troops were deploying flame throwers (*Flammenwerfen*) which could fire jets of fuel up to 25 metres. These weapons had a great demoralising effect on British troops and, when combined with other powerful weapons, proved mercilessly efficient at Hooge. German troops swiftly recaptured the area. The Germans continued to improve on the *Flammenwerfen* and used it many times during the remainder of the war. Though the Allies tinkered with it, they never really used flame throwers to any significant degree. Under the terms of the Treaty of Versailles it was one of the weapons, along with the submarine, battleship, heavy artillery, tank, Zeppelin and poison gas that Germany was forbidden to manufacture.

During 1916 the 7th Rifle Brigade was involved in the Battle of Delville Wood and Flers-Courcelette, both being part of the Battle of the Somme. Two weeks into the Battle of the Somme, after carnage on both sides, it became evident that neither side would break through to a decisive victory. What started to evolve was the individual capture of prominent towns, woods, or positions that would give either side a tactical advantage, including Deville Wood. The offensive started on 14 July and although it proved a tactical victory for the Allies, it was one of the bloodiest confrontations of the Somme, with both sides incurring large casualties.

The Battle of Flers-Courcelette came next, starting on 15 September. The offensive lasted a week and it was not a complete success, although the Allies did capture the villages of Courcelette, Flers and Martinpuich. The battle was significant for the very first use of tanks by the British in warfare and it was also the battle during which one of the authors' grandfathers, James Pitts, was injured, then subsequently repatriated.

The next major offensive the 7th Rifle Brigade was involved in was the Battle of Arras, from 9 April to 16 May 1917. This offensive involved a number of set battles, including:

- The First Battle of Scarpe (9-14 April)
- The Battle of Vimy Ridge (9-12 April)
- The First Battle of Bullecourt (10-11 April)
- The Battle of Lagnicourt (15 April)
- The Second Battle of Scarpe (23-24 April)
- The Battle of Arleux (28-29 April)
- The Second battle of Bullecourt (3-16 May)
- The Third Battle of Scarpe (3-4 May)

Up until this point, the opposing armies on the Western Front had been, for much of the time, at a stalemate. As a combined offensive, with a French offensive some 80 kilometres away, the Battle of Arras was intended to take the German-held high ground and end the war in forty-eight hours.

The Arras region is chalky and therefore easily excavated. Both sides, the Allies to a slightly greater extent, produced over 20 kilometres of tunnels, not only for mining but also for troop movements. The tunnel system had grown large enough to conceal 24,000 troops. The tunnels were used for more than the clandestine movement of troops, however, and were equipped with electric light, built kitchens and latrines. Medical centres were set up there and they were used to transport ammunition down the line on tramways and bring casualties back up.

By the end of the first two days of the Battle of Arras, the British gains were nothing short of spectacular by the standards of the time. When the battle officially ended on 16 May 1917, the British troops had made significant advances but had not achieved the major breakthrough they had anticipated. The British could have claimed it as a victory, but their progress was offset by the failure of the French to make any headway and the devastating losses: 150,000 Allied and British troops and 120,000–130,000 German troops.

It is difficult to ascertain in which of these battles Edward Depper was involved, yet he was possibly engaged at Inverness Copse, which was completely destroyed. There is no doubt, however, that Edward had performed with extreme courage throughout the battle. The *London*

Gazette reported on 30 October 1917 that he was to receive the Military Medal, which was awarded for acts of gallantry and devotion to duty under fire or for individual acts of bravery deemed insufficient to merit the Distinguished Conduct Medal. It appears that Edward was not satisfied with his Military Medal, however, because the *Chelmsford Chronicle* of 23 November 1917 notes that he had also been awarded the Distinguished Conduct Medal.

The news was also reported in the *London Gazette* on 6 February 1918:

> *For conspicuous gallantry and devotion to duty in command of his party after the officer had been killed, leading his men with great dash and personally killing several of the enemy. On returning to our trenches he carried back the body of his Officer under heavy machine fire.*

Then, on 18 January 1918, the *Chelmsford Chronicle* reports that, Sergeant E.E. Depper RB, the recipient of both the Distinguished Conduct and the Military Medal had an enthusiastic reception on his arrival at Canvey.

'The Soldier'
If I should die, think only this of me:
That there's some corner of a foreign field
That is for ever England. There shall be
In that rich earth a richer dust concealed;
A dust whom England bore, shaped, made aware,
Gave, once, her flowers to love, her ways to roam,
A body of England's, breathing English air,
Washed by the rivers, blest by suns of home.

And think, this heart, all evil shed away,
A pulse in the eternal mind, no less
Gives somewhere back the thoughts by England given;
Her sights and sounds; dreams happy as her day;
And laughter; learnt of friends; and gentleness,
In hearts at peace, under an English heaven.
                    (By Rupert Brooke, Died 23 April 1915)

Garnet Frederick Hester – After eighteen months of war young men were still signing up to take part in this gruesome conflict. One of them was Garnet Hester, the grandson of Frederick Hester whose vision it had been to make Canvey Island another Southend-on-Sea. As previously described, Frederick's grand plans unfortunately failed, but his family continued to live on the island and the 1911 census shows his son Frederick William Brewster, his wife Elizabeth and two sons Victor Leslie and Garnet Frederick living at 'St Omar', Winter Gardens, on Canvey Island. A few months later, Frederick William died and he was buried in St Katherine's Churchyard.

On 19 February 1916 Garnet Hester enlisted at Southend into the Rifle Brigade, 6th Reserve Battalion. He had registered his age as nineteen years and five months, but in reality he was still only sixteen. Garnet was sent to Winchester and while he was there his mother found out and contacted the brigade. Following the brigade's request for his birth certificate, she sent the following letter, dated 3 March 1916:

Dear Sirs,
I herewith enclose my son's certificate of birth, G.F. Hester S15984, 6th BRB. I have received the clothing belonging to somebody else, the initials on socks are W G, perhaps I had better send information to Winchester.

Trusting you do not think this cowardly of me, but my boy became infatuated by another boy joining at the same time. Thanking you in anticipation of my son's quick return.

I am yours faithfully,

Elizabeth Hester.

A few days later, she received the following letter, dated 5 March 1916, and a similar letter was also sent to the commanding officer of 'D' Company:

To: Mrs Elizabeth Hester,
With further references to exchanged correspondence re your son No. S15984 Rifleman Garnet Hester.
Birth certificate is returned herewith and your son being under the age of 17 years can be discharged from the service.

Before, however, his discharge can be proceeded with it will be necessary for him to provide himself with a suit of plain clothes and be in possession of sufficient money to enable him to pay his own fare home and he has been so informed.

Lieutenant, 6th Reserve Battalion.

Garnet was discharged on 15 March 1916. Whatever reception he received on his return home, it did not deter him from his military ambitions, because as soon as he was of age he re-enlisted into the East Kent Regiment (The Buffs), and was later transferred to the Queen's Regiment. Other than his medal card, which shows he was awarded the Victory and British War Medals, no other service papers survive. Yet Garnet survived the war and returned to Canvey Island. He left the island in later life and married Marjorie Kay in 1931.

Garnet's older brother **Victor Leslie Hester** seems to have been equally adventurous, as on 21 May 1913 at the age of fifteen, he emigrated to Australia. He left aboard the ship *Belgic* from Liverpool and embarked at Fremantle. The Australian census of 1958 shows that he remained in Fremantle and later married, before he died in 1966.

South Benfleet Soldiers in the Great War:
Stanley Thomas Ellison is believed to have been the first South Benfleet man to be killed on the Western Front in the First World War and also possibly the first Castle Point casualty. He was born in Enfield on 15 May 1893 to Thomas Daniel and Alice Eliza Ellison and he enlisted at Mill Hill in 1912, with the Royal Engineers, 56th Field Company at the rank of Sapper.

Stanley seems to have been a hard-working, clean-living young man and his school report for September 1901 from Bush Hill Park Boys' School records that a Certificate of Merit was awarded to him for 'Regular Attendance, Progress and Good Conduct'. A year later, at the age of nine he joined the Band of Hope, a temperance organisation for working-class children, founded in Leeds in 1847. The organisation was formed to combat the consumption of alcohol amongst children, which had become a major social problem during the nineteenth century. All members were required to make a pledge, promising to totally abstain from drinking alcoholic beverages, which became known as 'signing the pledge'.

Len Hawkins, a local South Benfleet WW1 historian has in his possession documents given to him for safe-keeping by Stanley Ellison's sister Hilda. These papers give the impression that Stanley came from a very close-knit family, for example a 1913 Christmas card sent to Stanley by Hilda a year after he enlisted, includes a piece of lucky heather.

A sapper, often referred to as a pioneer or combat engineer, is a soldier who performs a wide range of military engineering duties such as bridge-building, laying or clearing minefields, demolition, the construction of trenches and roads. The sapper's main task was to assist the movement of the troops, but they were also trained to serve as infantry personnel in defensive and offensive operations.

Stanley Thomas Ellison. (Reproduced with kind permission of the Len Hawkins Collection)

On 23 August 1914 the first British confrontation took place against enemy forces on European soil, since the Battle of Waterloo in 1815. It became known as the Battle of Mons, often referred to as the 'Retreat from Mons'. Four divisions of the British Expeditionary Force (BEF) struggled with the German 1st Army over a 60 foot wide section of the Mons Canal in Belgium, near the French frontier.

The Battle started at 09:00, with the German guns opening fire on the British positions. Although the Germans had numerical advantage of two to one, they did not make effective use of it and the British regiments withstood six hours of shelling and infantry assault. Due to the retreat of the French 5th Army further along the line, the BEF was in danger of being surrounded by the German forces. A decision was made to withdraw as soon as possible and, by the time the battle ended after nine hours of combat, some 35,000 British soldiers had been involved, with a total of 1,600 casualties. As the Ellison family were to find out over a year later, one of the casualties that day was Stanley. His family knew nothing of his death at the time, however, believing him to be safe, as the day before the battle his mother received a letter saying that he was 'quite well'.

In the retreat, the engineer units were engaged in demolishing railway and road bridges. Captain Theodore Wright and Lance

Corporal Charles Jarvis both of the 57th Field Company won Victoria Crosses for their actions in demolishing bridges on the Mons-Conde Canal.

The 56th Field Company War Diary for the 23 August 1914 reads as follows:

> *Battle of Mons, Nos 1, 3 or 4 Section were ordered to prepare bridges on the canal from Nimy, eastwards for demolition. The work however was not to be carried out without the direct order of a staff officer 3rd Division. None of the Sections succeeded owing to finding the enemy in force at all the bridges.*
>
> *At the end of the day the Company retired to Nouvelles with the 8th Infantry Battalion and prepared a position for defence there during the night.*
>
> *The casualties on this day were Lieutenant Holt and twenty one N.C.Os and men missing and one wagon.*

Four months later, on 2 December Stanley's mother, unaware of his death sent him the following letter:

> *Dear Stanley,*
>
> *If this letter reaches you which I trust it will. Let me have a line if possible as we are all very anxious about you. Dad has written asking about you and of course I cannot send any news until I hear from you. Grandma and Amy are also anxious to have news of you.*
>
> *Fondest Love*
> *From Mother*
> *From Mrs Ellison.*

The letter was received by the Army Records Office Expeditionary Force in London. They marked the envelope 'Missing' and returned it. Naturally the family were very anxious but they continued to hope that he might turn up. In October 1915 the family finally received confirmation of his death in a letter from a former companion, Sapper E. Hargreaves. The news was reported in the *Southend Standard* and *Essex Weekly Advertiser*:

News has only recently come to hand respecting the death of Sapper Stanley Ellison of the Royal Engineers. Deceased was only 21 years of age and the son of Mr and Mrs Ellison of 'The Rosary' South Benfleet. Ellison joined the Royal Engineers some two years before the war was declared and went out with the first expeditionary force. On August 22nd 1914 he wrote to his mother stating he was quite well but unfortunately, the following day he met his death. He was however reported as being amongst the missing and his parents therefore were hoping that he might eventually turn up. No news was received concerning him for nearly fourteen months and then the sad intelligence was conveyed to his mother through a former companion of Ellison's who was present at his death.

Writing from a German internment camp Ellison's friend Sapper K. Hargreaves sent the following letter:

Dear Mrs Ellison
On 23 August 1914 your son went into action with me as a cyclist signaller at a place called Nimme near Mons and at 10 am., he received a bullet through the head, death being instantaneous. I was myself severely wounded at the same time and place but I am well again. The sad news I give you with great reluctance and I trust that you may bear up under the shock.

Sapper E Hargreaves

On 22 October 1915, the *Chelmsford Chronicle* also reported his death: 'Sapper Stanley Ellison, R.E., 21 years of age. Killed in action, was the son of Mr and Mrs Ellison, of 'The Rosary,' South Benfleet.'

After receiving the letter from Sapper Hargreaves, the Ellison family sent food parcels to him until he returned to England, and he later visited the family to thank them. Stanley's mother, as might be expected, was distraught with grief over her son's death and amongst her papers she kept the following poem she wrote following his death:

'A few lines from mother'
No last goodbyes
No anxious hours of watching
No pillow smoothed beneath the dying head
No tears upon the new turned earth that covers
Our honoured dead
Not thus God took him
But simply, swiftly passing
From sudden strife to sudden perfect peace
He entered to his heritage a conqueror
In that fair land where tears for ever cease.
He is not far away
Fear, nearer than when in
Awful warfare on strange soil
His spirit comes to us across our weeping
And mingles with our toil,
For him the glorious resurrection morning
For us to wait awhile and weep
Till, as he hails us through the coming dawning,
We wake, no more to sleep.

In 1920 the Ellison family received a Memorial Scroll from the Royal Engineers Record Office and at a later date the Memorial Plaque (known as the 'Dead Man's Penny'). The following year they also received his three medals, including the 1914 Star, with a clasp indicating that it was awarded under fire, as well as the Victory and British War Medals.

Also amongst the Ellison family's papers is a Royal Engineers cap badge and a small memorial badge, possible worn by Stanley's mother: 'In loving memory of Sapper S Ellison R.E. Mons.'

In 1927 the family received a letter from the Imperial War Graves Commission, requesting 7 shillings for the cost of a personal inscription engraved on Stanley's headstone, which was raised at his burial place in Hautrage Military Cemetery. The inscription at the bottom of the headstone reads: 'NOW THE LABORER'S TASK IS O'ER', a quote from the 1875 hymn by John Ellerton:

Stanley Ellison's medals. (Reproduced with kind permission of the Len Hawkins Collection)

Now the Laborer's task is o'er;
Now the battle day is past;
Now upon the farther shore;
Lands the voyager at last.

Refrain
Father, in Thy gracious keeping
Leave we now Thy servant sleeping.
Etc.

Hautrage Military Cemetery is in a pine wood, south-east of the village of Hautrage in the Province of Hainaut, Belgium, just 9 miles west of Mons. The village was in German hands for most of the war and the cemetery was constructed by the Germans in August and September 1914. Then, in the summer of 1918, British graves of 1914

Stanley Ellison's Grave at Hautrage Military Cemetery.
(Reproduced with the kind permission of the Len Hawkins
Collection)

were transferred to the cemetery from surrounding battlefields and
local cemeteries. After the Armistice a further twenty-four graves were
brought in from other cemeteries.

The 56th also lost 2nd Lieutenant Wilfred H. Holt and Sapper F. Johnson on 23 August 1914, but the first man from the company to have died on the Western Front was Private John Parr of the 4th Battalion of the Middlesex Regiment, who was killed while on patrol on 21 August. Stanley and many thousands of others may have survived if, instead of the army-issue peaked cloth cap, they had had the Brodie Helmet or 'Tommy's Helmet' as it became known, but these protective helmets did not become available until the spring of 1916. The peaked cloth cap was a serious weakness in the British Army uniform and there is no doubt that it was one of the major reasons why so many men were killed in the early months of the war.

Stanley Thomas Ellison is commemorated on the South Benfleet War Memorial and, for a short time, he was also listed on his parents' grave in the churchyard, but in recent years this grave has been destroyed. An interesting footnote to Stanley's story is that the last British soldier killed in World War One shared his surname, although he does not seem to have been a relative. Private George Edwin Ellison of the 5th Royal Irish Lancers, was killed at Mons, where he had also fought in 1914. He died at 09:30, just 90 minutes before the ceasefire was announced.

Stanley Smith Pilbrow was born in 1874 to John and Hannah from Poplar. He got married in 1895 and, for a while, became a professional soldier. He was a veteran of the Boer War, serving with the Scottish Horse as a quartermaster sergeant. The regiment had been raised in the 1900s for service in the Second Boar War but records show that Stanley received a slightly different set of medals: the Queen's South Africa Medal (with clasps for time spent in Cape Colony, Orange Free State, Transvaal and South Africa) and the King's South Africa Medal. His records also note that he was discharged on 30 August 1901 for being inefficient.

Inefficient or not, the army did not hesitate to call him up on reserve in August 1914. Soon he was enlisted into the 2nd King Edward's Horse as a private trooper, stationed at Slough, Buckinghamshire. He was apparently a giant of a man, as the army struggled to find a greatcoat to fit him. After he caught a very bad cold from sleeping on the ground in tents during icy weather, he was sent to a Military Hospital, then returned home. But his condition worsened and he was taken to Bournemouth Hospital, where he died on 9 December 1915. At the time of his death Stanley's family were living in South Benfleet and he had a son serving in the Shropshire Light Infantry.

Stanley is buried in Sutton Road Cemetery, Southend and he is commemorated on the South Benfleet War Memorial and in the Southend Roll of Honour.

'In Hospital'
We from the sunless, airless trench,
The Mud, the muddy bread, the stench,
Of no Man's Land, where English, French,
And Germans rest,

Came on an English April day
Through sun-filled railway-cuttings, gay
With English primroses, away
Into the West,

And found ourselves with Plymouth Sound
Beneath us and Drake's bowling-ground
Above; and from the heights around
The bay there came

The boom of English guns, the call
Of English bugles. Best of all,
In this kind Devon hospital,
The old, the same

Strong gentleness of nursing eyes
And mothering hearts and hands that bring
Health radiant as an English spring
To wounded, sick and suffering.
    (By Charles Edward Montague, died in 1928)

Harold Francis Box was born in Orsett in 1895, the son of Reverend Charles Francis and Emily Box. At the time of the 1911 census the family was living at the vicarage in South Benfleet, where the Reverend was the local rector. Harold attended Keble College, Oxford and it was his intention to follow in his father's footsteps and take Holy Orders.

However, in early 1915 he obtained a commission in the Essex Regiment, 5th Battalion, before transferring to the Royal Engineers, reaching the rank of captain. He was killed a few days before the Armistice, on 29 October 1918. His Commanding Officer reported that during his war service Harold had done some excellent work with the Signalling Company on the Western Front and spoke of him in the highest terms: 'His bright and cheerful manners, with his generous and kindly disposition, made him a great favourite with all his men.'

Harold was killed while he was asleep in a temporary bivouac, in a front trench near Valenciennes which was hit by a shell. He was buried by the side of the officer with whom he had shared the dugout and his resting place is in the village cemetery near Valenciennes. His mother Emily was living in Brighton at the time of his death, his father having passed away. He was posthumously awarded the Victory and British War Medals and is commemorated on the South Benfleet War Memorial and the Church Memorial. Harold's elder brother also joined the Royal Engineers as a lieutenant, but he survived the war and returned to his mother in Brighton, where he later got married.

Hadleigh Soldiers in the Great War

The village of Hadleigh offers an intriguing, yet undocumented soldier's story. It appeared in the *Essex Newsman* on 1 January 1916, under the column 'On the Field of Honour':

> **Pathetic story of an old Hadleigh Colonist:**
> *The Salvation Army has issued, under the title 'Won!' a brief account of some aspects of its remarkable work against poverty, misery and crime during the year. From this booklet we take the following pathetic story.*
>
> *What higher duty can a man undertake than to conquer himself, or help others to reformation of character? Even the heart of the Government, which is usually filled with intentions of strict justice was touched to pity by Norman Hudder. Committed to penal servitude for a very serious crime, he remained for many years in prison.*
>
> *All the long-service officials knew him. Year after year slipped away, going with leaden feet in the cells where each hour was a day and there was always Hudder, the convict,*

in the same place, shut away from society he had horrified, doing the same tasks, seeing the same strip of sky and square of walls during 'exercise.'

What had really happened to the man who was Hudder, who lived inside his body and thought and felt like other men, nobody troubled to guess but after his crime and imprisonment, he was docile, careful, obedient, meek. Hudder never gave the warders trouble. He was a prisoner but a gentler, quieter prisoner could not be.

'No 0924 has been here a lifetime. Look up his papers and report to me,' said the new Governor after some months of his reign.

There were no faults mentioned in the prison record. It was remarkable. 'We'll let the Salvation Army have him,' decided the authorities later. 'They will guard him and he may have a spell of something like ordinary life before he dies. Write to General Booth.'

The General received the letter and replied. Hudder found himself passed from a warder, who said with astounding feeling on parting, 'Goodbye, 0924, You've done your best to wipe out, if ever man did. I hope you'll get on.'

A Salvation Army Officer, who took his hand – Hudder had forgotten how to shake hands – said, 'God bless you!' You belong to us now, It's all in the family!'

In bed, a real bed, at the Land and Industrial Colony, Hadleigh, Essex, that night, Hudder wept. It was so long since he had shed a tear, that he sat up and cried child-fashion, weeping loudly and pitifully. A Salvationist came and put an arm round his neck and Hudder wept away the hidden misery of years.

How he worked! I saw him once loading hay on one of the Colony's wains and never forgot it, or the sight of his face, tanned and healthy now but such a face of man as I had rarely seen and am not likely to see again, wholly free from judgement of anybody and full of grateful kindness to all. Ah, Hudder, a violent temper, walking in the road that day by the field, prayed God such victory might be given-as He gives to you!

Hudder was converted then. With the permission of the authorities, he afterwards went to a situation and his conduct and service were exemplary...War Came...

The soldier that had been Hudder before he was a convict, sprang to arms and would not be denied. He joined the King's Army. He became a sergeant. He went to France and the Front.

'My trust is still in God,' said each letter that came from him to his family – The Salvation Army. 'My trust is still in God.' repeated a pencilled note received at the end of January 1915.

In February he was killed in action, fighting for the Old Land, whose laws he had broken and whose heavy punishment he had borne. 'Somewhere in France' he lies in death, one among the noble host who yielded their lives that the Old Land might be the Old Land still.

Peace to him! Many a man has a more ignoble history. The Salvation Army has no tears for Hudder, late 0924. His sins were forgiven the White Comrade must have met him there on the battlefield and taken himself the soul. He died to save. The vast family of all nations, called The Salvation Army, owns Hudder – 'One of Ours'.

Hudder may have been one of the hundred men from the Hadleigh Salvation Army colony who enlisted in the British Army.

Harold Clifford was employed as a Foreman at the Salvation Army Colony at the time he enlisted with the 11th Battalion, Royal Sussex Regiment in June 1916. He was born in 1883 in Battersea and married Florence Winifred (née Smith) in 1914. At the time he enlisted, Harold's battalion was already in France and had already seen a considerable amount of action on the Western Front in 1916. Harold probably missed the majority of the 1916 action but the battalion was soon in the thick of it once more, at the Battle of Pilckem Ridge (31 July–2 August 1917), the opening attack of the main part of the Third Battle of Ypres. This was soon followed with the Battle of Langemarck (16–17 August).

Between these various offensives, periodic shelling of the trenches continued on both sides. Harold was killed while he was on duty as an observation scout, when a shell burst near him in the trench along with five others. The *Essex Newsman* reported his death on 6 October 1917:

> *Mrs Clifford of Arnewood, Rectory Road, Hadleigh, is informed that her husband, Sgt. Harold Clifford, Royal Sussex Regiment, has been killed by the bursting of a shell. Deceased was formerly Foreman at the Colony Nurseries. He was 35.*

Harold was buried at Zillebeke, Ypres, but his body has never been found. His officer wrote: 'He has worked closely with me for the last seven months as sniping and intelligence N.C.O., and as an observer scout, his reputation went beyond the Battalion.' He was entitled to the Victory and British War Medals and he is commemorated on the Tyne Cot Memorial and Hadleigh War Memorial.

The Choppen Family at War:
The Choppen family had lived in the Hadleigh and Thundersley area for several generations, with members of the family recorded as local wheelwrights, blacksmiths and one, Stephen Choppen, became the licensed victualler of the Castle Inn. Stephen's grandson, also Stephen, was the son of Harry (Henry) and Frances Choppen of 'Ashburnham', Church Road, Hadleigh.

Stephen Choppen the younger was employed as a plasterer, before he enlisted at Southend in the early days of the war. He joined the Essex Regiment, 9th Battalion and was promoted to Lance Corporal. The 9th, after nine months of training and hard work was finally prepared for war and left England for France, departing for Le Havre on 29 May 1915. The 9th Battalion had become part of the 12th Division and, after several months of getting accustomed to trench life and carrying out various reconnoitring patrols, they were involved in the Loos Offensive on 25 September 1915.

The Loos Offensive was a joint operation with the French, however any early gains made by the Allies could not be exploited, as reserves had been held too far back and failed to reach the Front Line in time. The 12th Division was not involved in the initial attack, but the 9th were involved in a diversionary attack, as the extract from the Regimental War Diary makes clear:

The Loos Offensive. (Reproduced with kind permission of the Len Hawkins collection)

25 September 1915

At 5.55am simultaneously with the launching of French and British attacks at various places south of Armentieries, at Hooge and in camp Champagne a curtain of smoke was raised to conceal our parapet along the whole of the front. It was preceded at 5am by an artillery shoot on enemy lines. Bundles of wet straw soaked in paraffin were lighted and thrown over our parapet, a bundle to every yard. Smoke bombs were thrown by hand and by the West thrower. A dense cloud of smoke was thus raised in a few minutes, rising to a height of 50 feet and drifting slowly toward enemy lines, the wind being favourable.

A similar procedure was followed by the battalions on our flanks. The enemy appeared considerably alarmed, a bell was heard ringing and maxim fire opened on our parapet to which our four machine guns replied and following the firing of a red rocket his artillery opened steady fire on our fire and support trenches and supporting points, with 7.7, 10.5 and 15cm shrapnel and HE shells. Laurence Farm East was struck by a 15cm HE and set on fire and burned to the ground, a number of packs and material lost. The enemy shooting was accurate, several direct hits on our trenches causing a score of casualties. In all about 130 shells were fired to which our artillery replied.

The months that followed saw the 9th moving backwards and forwards, from the trenches back behind the lines in reserve billets and during this period they were involved in a number of skirmishes. On 22 April 1916 the battalion moved into reserve at Bethune and then marched to billets at Raimbert, where a surprise inspection by the Brigadier judged the 9th the best turned out and awarded the battalion a prize. During their stay at Raimbert, Stephen Choppen was killed. The 9th casualty list for May 1916 recorded, 'No Officers – 2 Other Ranks, one died of wounds, one accidentally killed.' Stephen was the latter soldier, killed by the accidental explosion of a grenade on 25 May 1916, aged twenty-one. He was awarded the 1914-15 Star, Victory and the British War Medals. He is buried at the Lapugnoy Military Cemetery, Nord-Pas-de-Calais, France and is remembered on the Hadleigh War Memorial.

His cousin **Fred Choppen**, the son of James and Maria Choppen of Church Road, Thundersley, was a dairyman before he joined the 7th King's Royal Rifle Corps as a rifleman. The 7th was formed in August 1914 as part of Kitchener's Army and came under the 41st Brigade in the 14th (Light) Division. After training at Aldershot, Grayshott and Bordon, the 7th landed at Boulogne on 19 May 1915. It would appear that Fred went over to France a little later, however, as there is no record of his presence in France until 3 August 1915.

He may have been involved in one of the bloodiest confrontations of the Somme, at the Battle of Delville Wood, but it was at the Battle of Flers-Courcelette, which commenced on 15 September 1916, that Fred lost his life. He is buried in the Thiepval Cemetery, Picardy, France and his name also appears on the memorial there and on the Hadleigh War Memorial. He was awarded the 1914-15 Star, Victory and the British War Medals.

Stephen had two brothers, **William and Sidney Choppen**. Sidney, the youngest, enlisted on 27 August 1914 at Shoeburyness, immediately after his eighteenth birthday, into the Royal Horse and Royal Field Artillery and was assigned to the 110th Battery. Prior to enlistment he had been a grocer's assistant. The 110th was attached to

24th Brigade within the 6th Division, They were equipped with Howitzer. It is possible that Sidney was also transferred at times to other Brigades

Sidney was appointed acting bombardier in November 1914 and then on 19 May 1915 he was officially promoted to Bombardier, the Royal Artillery equivalent of the Infantry rank of corporal. He was later promoted to Sergeant on 2 September 1918.

After the requisite period of training, Sidney embarked at Southampton on 1 June 1915, landing at Le Havre on 2 June 1915. He was awarded the Military Medal at some point, as well as the 1914-15 Star, Victory and the British War Medals. Sidney was demobbed in May 1919 and transferred to the reserves. He married in 1927.

The wartime story of the third and eldest Choppen brother, William, is less well documented and the authors have been unable to establish whether or not he enlisted.

Frederick Carter was among the under-age 'boy soldiers' who attempted to join up, despite being well under the initial required age of nineteen. He was born in Westcliff-on-Sea, around 1900, to Edward and Annie Carter. In 1911, along with his older brother Bertie, he was boarded out with Alice Wilkinson of Love Lane, Rayleigh. By the outbreak of war, he was living with William and Rebecca Snow of 'Ivydene', Short Road, Hadleigh. Somehow he managed to enlist at Southend, just before his fourteenth birthday and he joined the Rifle Brigade (The Prince Consort's Own) 10th Battalion. The *Essex Newsman* of 4 November 1916 reported: 'Hadleigh soldier, Rifleman Fred Carter, of the Rifle Brigade has been killed at the age of fifteen and a half.'

Frederick was killed in action on 3 September 1916. His battalion, the 10th (Service) Battalion, was part of Kitchener's Second New Army and joined the 59th Brigade, 20th (Light) Division. The battalion finalised its training in April 1915 at Stonehenge, around the time that Frederick enlisted. They landed at Boulogne, France on 21 July 1915 and their first engagement was the Battle of Mount Sorrel, in which the division, along with Canadian troops recaptured the Heights. Their next engagements were the Battle of Delville Wood, (1 July – 3 September 1916) and the Battle of Guillemont (3 September – 6 September 1916), part of the overall offensive during the Battle of the Somme.

It is likely to have been during the Battle of Guillemont that Frederick was killed. The offensive started with a bombardment in the early hours of the morning, followed by an infantry attack at noon. The attack which employed push-pipes and liquid fire, went well for the British troops, although as usual there were heavy casualties. The eastern side of the village was taken by 13:30, despite fierce hand-to-hand fighting within the village, which was finally secured the following day.

Frederick was awarded the Victory Medal posthumously, but it was returned unclaimed to the military in 1921. He is commemorated on the Hadleigh War Memorial. Guillemont Road Cemetery has 1,522 unmarked graves and Frederick's last resting place is likely to be among them.

Alfred Gilbert's death was reported by the *Chelmsford Chronicle* on 26 January 1917, as follows:

> *Mrs Gilbert of Lynton Road, Hadleigh has received notification that her husband, private Alfred Gilbert, Essex Regt., previously reported missing, is now presumed to have been killed on 6 August 1915, at Suvla Bay. He was a member of the Hadleigh Wesleyan Church, a class leader and local preacher and 36 years of age. He leaves a widow and four young children.*

Today is it difficult to imagine the uproar that would occur if it took nearly sixteen months to confirm a serviceman's death. We cannot fully understand what the Gilbert family and many others went through while they waited for news, hoping that their loved one was either in hospital or a prisoner of war.

Alfred Gilbert was born in Barningham, Suffolk in 1879 to Harry and Hortensia Gilbert. The 1911 census shows him living at 1 Fairview Villas, Lynton Road, Hadleigh, with his wife Mary Rebekah and their four children. When he enlisted at Warley on 2 December 1914, into the 1st Battalion, Essex Regiment, he had been working as groom and gardener for Mr Hughes of Woodcroft, Thundersley. Thomas Hughes was a factory manager at Ilford Ltd and his wife worked in the photographic department of the same company. They must have been

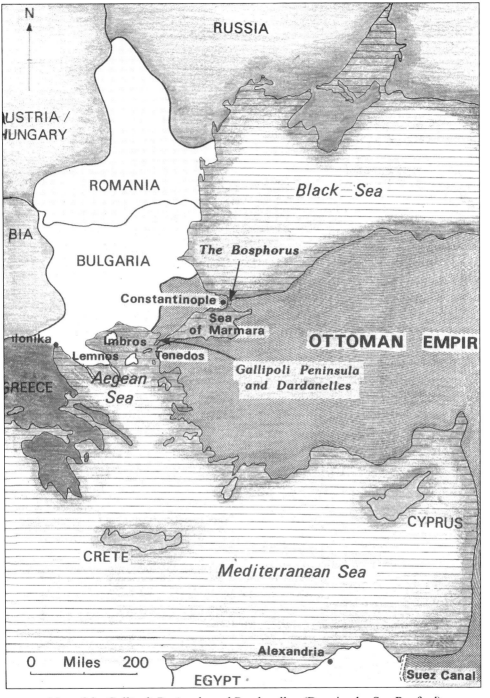

Map of the Gallipoli Peninsula and Dardanelles. (Drawing by Sue Ranford)

fairly well-off for the time, because in addition to Alfred they also employed a house maid and house boy.

The Suvla Bay landings were part of the Dardanelles offensive. The campaign came about when the Turks closed the Dardanelles to Allied shipping, following an incident where British troops had seized a Turkish torpedo boat. The Turkish fleet then began raiding the Russian fleet in the Black Sea, resulting in Russia declaring war on Turkey on 2 November 1914, followed by the British on 6 November. In response to Russia's request for help in the area, the British commenced naval bombardment in early February 1915.

The 1st Battalion landed at Gallipoli on 25 April 1915 and from that date onwards they saw a considerable amount of action. Alfred Gilbert had arrived on 10 June 1915, possibly at Gully Beach, before moving to the Front Line near Krithia on 13 June 1915 and participating in a successful advance into enemy territory. The battalion withdrew for a long rest on 11 July 1915, before returning to the Front Line, again near Krithia, where on 6 August 1915 the British launched another attack on Turkish positions at Helles and Anzac Cove. The attack was intended to be minor action, to divert attention from the imminent nearby Allied landings to the north at Suvla Bay.

A postwar account on what was later referred to as the Battle of Krithia Vineyard reported:

> *The Essex were detailed to attack the trenches H12a, H12 and trenches under construction north-east of H12 near Krithia. The artillery opened at 2.30p.m. but was replied to by the Turks with shrapnel and high explosives on the British trench system, particularly the reserve trenches, causing many casualties.*
>
> *At 3.50 p.m. the battalion advanced on two lines, two companies (Y and Z) moving in H12a from the south-west, having 200 yards to traverse before reaching the enemy's trenches. A third (W) attacked H12 and there connected with H12a, each company finding its own supports. X Company was in reserve. The movement on H12 was at first very successful. The position was taken with few casualties but very heavy shrapnel fire was opened as the men moved forward again. With great gallantry they took the next trench*

(H12a) but were then held up by machine-gun and rifle fire and bombs.

The companies were so weak that on the Turks counter-attacking with bomb and bayonet they were driven back to H12a and its approaches and then left to the corner of the Southern Barricade. The company on the left (W) reached the trench in continuation of the Southern Barricade and that leading north from it but were unable to secure the continuation of the Northern Barricade. In the section between the two Barricades, serious casualties were sustained, six officers alone being killed there.

At nightfall the Battalion had secured, as a result of much desperate fighting, the corner formed by H12 and the trench connecting that point and H12a, the only means of communication was a small tunnel under the Southern Barricade. Part of X Company was sent forward, with details of other companies, during the night, as the position was difficult to hold on account of it being exposed on three sides to enemy fire. The order had, however, been issued that the trench was to be held at all costs and the men did so, although suffering considerably from thirst, supplies reaching them by means of petrol tins. At daybreak on 7 August the battalion was moved out of the line to Gully Beach, having suffered very heavy casualties – killed, 50; missing, 180; wounded, 202; a total of 432.

While this fighting was going on, the landings at Suvla Bay started at 22:00 on the evening of 6 August, involving 63,000 Allied troops. There was virtually no Turkish opposition, other than sniper fire. The idea behind this landing was for fresh troops to link up with those attacking Helles and Anzac Cove and then make a complete sweep across the Gallipoli peninsula. Unfortunately, the troops could not break out of Anzac Cove and the British at Suvla were then pushed back by a frantic attack by the Turks.

Eventually, the government called for an end to the campaign and the evacuation from Suvla Bay and Anzac Cove took place on 19-20 December, followed by the evacuation of Hellas a few days later, all without any casualties. However, the overall campaign was a great disaster, with over 200,000 Allied casualties, many due to disease and an even greater number of Turkish deaths. According to newspaper reports, Alfred Gilbert was killed at Suvla Bay, but as the troops positioned there only experienced sniper fire, it is more likely that he was involved in the attack at Helles or at Anzac Cove, where there were at least 180 missing British soldiers.

The Southend Roll of Honour states that Alfred was killed at Cape Helles and was initially buried there. He was later reburied in Twelve Trees Copse Cemetery, Turkey. He was awarded the 1914/15 Star, the Victory and British War Medals and he is commemorated on the Hadleigh War Memorial.

Thundersley Parish Soldiers in the Great War:

Fred Cranness was born in Thundersley in 1895 to George and Elizabeth Cranness. The *Essex Newsman* of 29 September 1917 reported that Sergeant F. Cranness of the Essex Regiment had been awarded the Military Medal. In addition to the Military Medal, he was also awarded the 1914-15 Star, Victory and British War Medals.

Fred Cranness had enlisted into the 11th (Service) Battalion of the Essex Regiment on 4 October 1915. The 11th Battalion had been in France since August 1915 and Fred would have joined them sometime around March or April 1916. The Battalion's first major campaign of 1916 was the Battle of Flers-Courcelette, part of the Somme offensive, which commenced on 15 September 1916. This was followed by the Battle of Morval and the Battle of Le Transloy. In 1917 the Battalion saw action at Hill 70 and at Cambrai. In 1918 they were involved at the Battle of St Quentin, the Battle of Lys, Battles of the Hindenburg Line and the pursuit to the Selle.

The Battle of Selle (17–26 October, 1918) was fought during the period that is now referred to as 'The Last Hundred Days of World War One'. There had been a six-day lull in fighting, allowing the British to prepare for the artillery bombardment, which began at 2:20 on 17 October, forcing the German troops to retreat. Fred Cranness would have seen a great deal of action with the 11th Battalion and during his service he earned the Military Medal. He was eventually discharged on 26 February 1919 and returned home to Thundersley, where he was still living in 1929.

Frederick William Hopwood enlisted into the Royal West Kent Regiment in 1915 and was sent to France in May 1916. He was promoted to Sergeant, then commissioned 2nd Lieutenant in early 1918 and attached to the 8th Battalion of the Royal Berkshire Regiment. The 8th Battalion served in France and Flanders, taking part in many major battles, including Loos in late 1915, the Somme in 1916 and Ypres in 1917. In 1918 they fought on the Somme and in the Battles of the Hindenburg line. Frederick was wounded twice and on the second occasion at Vimy Ridge he won the Military Medal. He was killed aged just 21, while leading his men into action on 27 August 1918, possibly in the action along the Hindenburg Line.

William Frederick Hopwood. (Photograph from the Southend Standard)

Frederick was the second son of Mr and Mrs Hopwood of 4 Orchard Cottages, Common Lane, Thundersley. His elder brother Private A.J. Hopwood was, at the time, serving with the Machine Gun Corps and his father, also Frederick William, had served with the Army Veterinary Corps for three years in Salonika and was in Marseilles at the time of his son's death. The Army Veterinary Corps was responsible for the medical care of animals, predominantly horses, mules and pigeons. Although fully trained, its members were only expected to use their weapons in self-defence.

One of Frederick Hopwood's fellow officers wrote of him:

> *Second Lieutenant Hopwood was shot in the head whilst gallantly leading his men into action. A more right royal gallant lad no one could wish to have fighting by his side. He will be especially missed by his platoon and the whole battalion sends sympathy.*

A memorial service was held for him in October 1918, attended by his brother and fiancée, who was working as a VAD in Overcliff Hospital. Frederick is buried at Quarry Cemetery, Montauban, the only soldier from the Royal Berkshire Regiment to be buried there. He is commemorated on St Peter's, Church, Thundersley, Roll of Honour Memorial and in addition to the Military Medal he was awarded the Victory and British War Medals.

The Pond Family at War:
The 1911 census shows Alfred and Alice Pond living in Church Road, Thundersley with their eleven children: three girls and eight boys. They must have been very worried when war broke out, because at least six of the boys would, at some time during the duration of the war, be eligible for call-up. As it turned out, only two of the Pond boys are recorded as having enlisted.

The 1929 Electoral Register shows Alfred and Alice living at 'Hill Top' in Hart Road, Thundersley with four of their sons, Harold, Edward, Henry who would all have been eligible for war service and James who was not. Intriguingly, two more are missing: Alfred, who would have been eligible to go to war and John, who was too young to be called up.

Arthur Edwin Pond was the second son of Alfred and Alice and, at the time of the 1911 census he was working as an assistant butcher. He enlisted at Southend in September 1914 into the Essex Regiment, 9th battalion, 'D' Company. He was promoted to Lance Corporal and sent with his battalion to the front in August 1915, where he took part in the fighting at Hill 60 and Loos.

Hill 60 consisted of man-made spoils from a nearby railway cutting and as it proved an invaluable vantage point from which to view the wider battlefield, Hill 60 changed hands several times during the war. A great deal of the fighting around the Hill was underground and it is understood that the first British mine of the war was detonated beneath it. Even when there was no direct assault on the Hill, there were still constant skirmishes going on and during one of these Arthur would have had his first taste of warfare. He had been in France only six weeks before he was killed by a shell at Vermelles on 13 October 1915, after having already been wounded twice.

On the evening of 5 October the 9th Battalion were marched to rest at Vermelles Halte. Whilst there, the enemy forcefully counter attacked, causing heavy casualties. A fierce British night attack followed, which included the 9th Battalion. The various Battalions were relieved by the 15th Scottish Division, enabling them to retire and rest at Fouquières-lès-Béthune. On 12 October the 9th paraded and moved up into the Old British Line, in preparation for the operation the next day.

The following is an extract from the official report that appeared in the *Colonist* on 14 October 1915:

> *Yesterday afternoon, after a bombardment, we attacked the enemy trenches under cover of a cloud of smoke and gas from a point about 600 yards south-west of Hulluch to Hohenzollern Redoubt. We gained about 1,000 yards of Trenches just south and west of Hulluch but were unable to maintain our position there, owing to the enemy's shell fire. South-west of St. Elie we captured and held enemy's trenches behind the Vermelles-Hulluch road and on south-western edge of quarries, both inclusive.*

Arthur Pond was twenty-five years old when he was killed and, although he had only been in France for a very short time, he was awarded the 1914-1915 Star, Victory and British War Medals. He is commemorated on the Loos Memorial and the St Peter's Church Memorial in Thundersley.

Frederick Charles Pond was the fourth son of Alfred and Alice, born in Tottenham in 1898. He was educated in Thundersley and prior to enlisting he was employed as a mechanic. Frederick initially enlisted with the Royal Army Service Corps, at Grove Park in March 1917, then was transferred to the 16th Training Battalion, before ending up in the King's Royal Rifle Corps, 2nd Battalion as a Rifleman. He was sent to France in June after three months' training.

Frederick Charles Pond. (Photograph from the *Southend Standard*)

His stay in France was a little longer than that of his brother Arthur, as it was some five months before he died of wounds on 10 November 1917, at St Julien, north-east of Ypres during the second Battle of Passchendaele, which was part of the Third Battle of Ypres. The objective of the battle was to capture favourable observation positions and gain drier winter positions on higher ground. The final action took place on 10 November in the vicinity of Hill 52 and it was noted as an Allied victory. Yet the Allied troops did not quite achieve all the ground they had hoped to gain, because additional divisions had to be sent to the Italian Front, where the Germans had inflicted a decisive defeat on the Italian Army at the Battle of Caporetto.

The *Essex Newsman* of 24 November 1917 reported Frederick Pond's demise:

> *The death occurred from wounds on 10 November of Rifleman Fredk. C. Pond, King's Royal Rifles, fourth son of Mr and Mrs Pond, of Hilltop, Thundersley. The Deceased, who was 19 years of age, was a native of Thundersley and subsequently he was employed on the Red Motor Buses running between Hadleigh and Leigh and later at Kynoch's garage, Southend.*

Frederick is buried at Duhallow ADS Cemetery, West Flanders, Belgium and is commemorated on St Peter's Church War Memorial, along with his brother. He was awarded the Victory and British War Medals. Frederick's commanding officer wrote to his family after his death: 'He tried more than all the rest and made a good soldier.' He was nineteen years old when he died.

Samuel Sargent was born in 1899 at Rawreth, Essex to Samuel and Eliza Sargent. He was educated at Hadleigh Council School and subsequently employed by Mr Ruggins, a poultry farmer of Kiln Road, Thundersley. He enlisted at Warley in March 1917 into the York and Lancaster Regiment, 3/13th (1st Barnsley) Battalion, at the rank of Private. This was a strange battalion for Samuel to be enlisted with, as it was a Pals Battalion formed by the South Yorkshire town of Barnsley.

After at least three months of training, he was sent to France to join the 13th, but was invalided home in October 1917 suffering from trench foot. Trench foot is an infection that is caused when the feet are immersed in cold and wet conditions for a prolonged period of time. This was very prevalent in the First World War, because soldiers were unable to remove their boots and socks to dry or air their feet. The foot steadily becomes numb, turning red or blue and, if it is not treated, the foot can eventually turn gangrenous, which can lead to amputation.

'Tommy's Dwelling'

I come from trenches deep in slime,
Soft slime so sweet and yellow,
And rumble down the steps in time
to souse 'some shivering fellow'.

I trickle in and trickle out
Of every nook and corner,
And, rushing like some waterspout,
Make many a rat a mourner.

I gather in from near and far
A thousand brooklets swelling,
And laugh aloud a great 'Ha, ha!'
To flood poor Tommy's dwelling.
(By Harold Parry, died 6 May 1917.)

Samuel Sargent may have taken part in the 13th's final engagement, the Capture of Oppy Wood on 28 June 1917, before falling victim to trench foot. He did not return to France until 2 April 1918. By that time, the first Battle of Arras had already started and it would appear that Samuel was sent into action immediately. He was killed ten days later, on 12 April, aged nineteen. On the same day the British commander-in-chief, Field Marshal Sir Douglas Haig, issued an order prohibiting any further retreat: 'With our backs to the wall and believing in the justice of our cause, each one must fight on to the end.' The call to arms worked and British resistance hardened.

In the meantime, Samuel Sargent's mother received the following letter from Rev. John Calderbeck:

No doubt you have already heard the sad news of your son's death, Private S. Sargent, but I wish to join with my brother officers and men in forwarding our deepest sympathy with you in your sad bereavement. After we came out from the fighting on the Somme we only had a few days rest before we were sent north to take part in the new offensive which had commenced. We arrived at our destination early one morning and in the same evening made a successful counter attack but unfortunately, your son and a number of his comrades lost their lives as we were going over to take the position.

The place where your son fell was in the neighbourhood of a cluster of buildings called _____ [censored], which is some little distance east of the village of_____ [censored]. We mourn with you in the loss of another brave comrade who has laid down his life for all we hold most dear but we pray that the sacrifice of all the gallant comrades will not have been in vain. Our hearts go out to you in your great sorrow And we pray God's blessing be with you in all your sad bereavement.

Samuel is commemorated on the Ploegsteert Memorial to the Missing in Belgium and on the South Benfleet War Memorial. At the time of his death, his mother was living at 7 The Avenue, Kiln Road, Thundersley, and his father had already passed away. He was entitled to the Victory and British War Medals.

'When the Last Long Trek is Over'

When the last long trek is over,
And the last long trench filled in,
I'll take a boat to Dover,
Away from all the din;
I'll take a trip to Mendip
I'll see the Wiltshire downs,
And all my soul I'll then dip
In peace no trouble drowns.

Away from noise of battle,
Away from bombs and shells,
I'll lie where browse the cattle,
Or pluck the purple bells.
I'll lie among the heather,
And watch the distant plain,
Through all the summer weather,
Nor go to fight again.

(By Alec de Candole, died 4 September 1918.)

These are just a few of the many amazing stories of the south-east Essex men who took part in this devastating war. In the end 182 are believed to have died from the four parishes, and there may be more.

Common Medals Awarded During the First World War

- **The 1914 Star (Mons Star)** was awarded for service in France or Flanders (Belgium) between 5 August and 22 November 1914.
- **The 1914-15 Star** was awarded for service in France or Flanders (Belgium) between 23 November 1914 and 31 December 1915, or for service in any theatre between 5 August 1915 and 31 December 1915.
- **The Allied Subjects Medal** was awarded to individuals for service to the Allied cause, for example, helping British prisoners of war to escape.
- **The Allied Victory Medal (Victory Medal)** was awarded for service in any operational theatre between 5 August 1914 and 11 November 1914. It was issued to individuals who also received the 1914 or 1914-15 Stars and to most individuals who were issued with the British War Medal. The medal was also awarded for service in Russia from 1919-1920 and post-war mine clearance in the North Sea from 1918-1920.
- **The British War Medal** was awarded to both servicemen and civilians who either served in a theatre of war or served overseas between 5 August 1914 and 11 November 1918. It was also awarded for service in Russia and post-war mine clearance in the Baltic, the Black Sea and the Caspian Sea between 1919 and 1920.
- **The Distinguished Conduct Medal (DCM)** was awarded to non-commissioned officers for bravery.
- **The Distinguished Flying Cross (DFC)** was awarded to personnel of the Royal Air Force and other services and formerly to officers of other Commonwealth countries, for 'an act or acts of valour, courage or devotion to duty whilst flying in active operations against the enemy.'

- **The Distinguished Flying Medal (DFM)** was awarded to personnel below commissioned ranks of the Royal Air Force and other services and formerly also to personnel of other Commonwealth countries, for 'an act or acts of valour, courage or devotion to duty whilst flying in active operations against the enemy.'
- **The Distinguished Service Order (DSO)** was generally awarded to officers ranked Major and above for distinguished war service.
- **The Mercantile Marine War Medal** was awarded by the Board of Trade of the United Kingdom to members of the Merchant Navy for undertaking one or more voyages through a war or danger zone during the conflict.
- **The Military Cross Medal (MC)** was awarded to commissioned officers of the rank of Captain and below, as well as Warrant Officers, for valour during active operations.
- **Military Medal (MM)** was awarded to other ranks for bravery in land battle.
- **The Silver War Badge (SWB)** was awarded to servicemen who became ill or wounded while serving in a theatre of war or at home.
- **The Territorial Force War Medal** was awarded to servicemen who were members of the Territorial Force either on or before 30 September 1914 and who served in an operational theatre abroad between 5 August 1914 and 11 November 1918.
- **The Victoria Cross Medal (VC)** was awarded for valour in the face of the enemy.
- **Mention in Despatches** was an award for commendable service or bravery. Despatches were official reports which detailed military operations. Servicemen who had performed noteworthy actions were often mentioned in these reports.

CHAPTER 7

Victory and its Aftermath

The Armistice was signed on Monday, 11 November 1918. That afternoon the *Daily Telegraph* newspaper's headline proclaimed :

WORLD WAR IS OVER

Beaten Germany Accepts Armistice terms and Hostilities Cease on All Fronts. Mons taken by British as news reaches Army.

Prime Minister Lloyd George announced that the cessation of hostilities was effective at 11am on all fronts of Europe.

There were impromptu celebrations across the country; Big Ben rang out for the first time since 1914 and across the country church bells pealed, air raid sirens were set off, car horns were honked. That evening, Hadleigh's Parish Church was crowded for a special service and the organist Mr C.E. Judd played the National Anthems of all the Allies. Services were also held in the Congregational and Wesleyan Churches, (with an additional service in the Baptist Church two days later) followed by a big bonfire in the High Street.

The Armistice had come out of three days of intense negotiations in a rail siding of Compiègne. Due to the social upheaval in Germany

Victory March in London, July 1919. (Postcard)

at the time, the German Government in Berlin ordered the German delegation to sign the terms put on the table by the Allies at any cost.

The terms were set out as follows:

- Allies to Occupy Mainz, Cobleaz and Cologne
- U-boats to surrender.
- Battleships to be disarmed and Heligoland held as a Guarantee.
- Immediate evacuation of Belgium, Alsace-Lorraine and Luxembourg and repatriation of all inhabitants of these lands, within 11 days.
- Evacuation by enemy of Rhine lands completed within 16 days.
- Railways of Alsace-Lorraine to be handed over.
- All hidden mines and delay-action fuses to be revealed by German Command, who shall help in their destruction.
- Positions of poisoned wells, springs, etc., to be disclosed, under penalty of reprisals.
- All German troops in Russia, Rumania, and elsewhere to be withdrawn.
- Immediate repatriation of Allied and United States prisoners.
- Return of German prisoners to be settled by Peace Conference (but the release of those interned in Holland and Switzerland to continue).

- Repatriation of Allied civilians within one month.
- Complete abandonment of the Treaties of Bucharest and Brest-Litovsk.
- Unconditional evacuation of all German forces in East Africa within one month.
- Reparation for all damage done. No removal of material that affords security or pledge for recovery of losses.
- Immediate restitution of cash deposits in National Bank of Belgium and all stocks, shares and money removed.
- Restoration (to Allies in trust) of Russian or Rumanian gold yield to, or taken by, Germany.
- Immediate cessation of all hostilities at sea.
- Handing over to Allied and United States of all submarines.
- Six battle cruisers, 10 battleships, 8 light cruisers, 50 destroyers and other services to be disarmed.
- If, owing to mutinies, these ships are not handed over, the Allies reserve right to occupy Heligoland as a defence base to enforce terms of armistice.
- All Allied merchant ships in German hands to be delivered.
- Existing blockade conditions set up by Allies to be unchanged and all German merchant ships at sea to remain liable to capture.
- All Black Sea ports to be evacuated and warships seized by Germany to be handed over to Allies.
- Allies to have freedom of access to Baltic, with power to occupy German ports there. Germany to evacuate Belgian coastal ports. Duration of the armistice to be 36 days.
- 5,000 guns, (2,500 heavy, 2500 field guns), 30,000 machine guns. 300 minenwerfers (mine launchers), 2,000 aeroplanes, 5,000 locomotives, 150,000 wagons, 5,000 motor lorries to be handed over.
- Germans to retire beyond the Rhine.
- Rhine strategical bridges to be occupied as well as German territory west of the Rhine.
- The evacuation by German armies on the left bank of the Rhine.
- This territory shall be administered by local authorities under the control of the Allied and United States Armies of occupation.

- The occupation of these territories will be carried out by Allied garrisons, holding the reciprocal crossings of the Rhine at Mainz, Coblenz and Cologne, together with the bridgeheads at those points for a thirty kilometre range on the right bank.
- An industrial zone shall be set up on the right bank of the Rhine between the river and the line drawn between the Dutch and Swiss frontiers.
- In the case of inhabitants of the neutral zone no person shall be prosecuted for having taken part in military measures previous to the signing of the armistice.
- There shall be no evacuation of inhabitants; no damage or harm shall be done to the persons or property of the inhabitants.
- Military establishments of all kinds shall be delivered intact, as well as military stores and food, within the period fixed for the evacuation.

Germany signed these tough peace terms on 28 June 1919. The Armistice initially ran for thirty-six days but was regularly renewed until the formal peace treaty was signed at Versailles. Should the Germans have deviated in any way from the terms of the Armistice, the Allies warned that a resumption of hostilities would begin within forty-eight hours. Further peace treaties were signed between the Allied and Austria in September 1919, Bulgaria in November 1919, Turkey (the Ottoman Empire) in April 1920 and Hungary in June 1920. By this time, the new map of Europe and the Balkans had emerged.

The British Prime Minister, David Lloyd George, promised that his coalition government would make Britain 'a land fit for heroes to live in.' There is no doubt that, initially, the soldiers who came back from the trenches received the thanks of a grateful country. A suit of civilian clothes, a set of medals and a small cash payment were supplied to them. The men who had stayed behind on the Home Front, however, were by and large, a lot better off than the ex-soldiers, as they had stable jobs and a home life uninterrupted by war service. There were also contradictory feelings at work, as many of those returning from the trenches wanted to forget the horrors, while those who had lost loved ones did not want to forget them.

Spanish Flu was still rampant for months after the war had ended and within a couple of years there was a huge economic recession. Unemployment was high, beggars appeared on the streets and it seemed that the gratitude of the country towards its former soldiers was rapidly running out. In August 1919, at South Benfleet a soldier was evicted from the cottage his wife had rented back in May 1918.

At South Benfleet on Saturday 18 August the police were required to carry out an ejectment order issued by the Justices, who had allowed a month's grace. In May 1918, a cottage was taken by Mrs Todd, the wife of a Marine, with three children. Mr Todd was demobilised on 29 April last. The ejectment order was obtained by the owner of the cottage on the ground that the place was required by an employee. Mr and Mrs Todd unsuccessfully tried to find another place, so all their goods and chattels were placed by the police at the side of the road and father, a mother, in a delicate state of health and three children, the eldest of whom is only five and a half, were homeless. Todd has had seventeen years service with the colours and he served at Ostend, Dunkirk, Antwerp, Gallipoli and on armed merchant ships.

However, elsewhere things were slowly improving: sports clubs were springing up again; various events, such as horticultural shows, were beginning to flourish again. Ex-servicemen were being invited to special entertainments. Hadleigh, in September 1919, entertained about fifty ex-servicemen at a dinner and concert held at the Castle Hotel. A Mr C. Clark presided over the dinner, at which Lieutenant Ellwood, RFA, in reply to the toast of 'HM Forces,' commented that Hadleigh took a high place among the south-east Essex villages in the matter of sending men to war and there had not been one conscientious objector from the village. Lieutenant Ellwood was obviously not fully informed of the facts, because Hadleigh had at least one local conscientious objector in Murray Cecil Frost. A Mr R. Morris also referred in feeling terms to the forty-seven men of Hadleigh who had given their lives in the war.

Ex-soldiers also received recognition within the Representation of the People Act of 1918, which marked a major social change in Britain. Men over the age of 21 could now vote without having a property qualification and women could at last vote, but only if they were aged over 30 and met certain property qualifications. This Act resulted in the size of the British electorate tripling overnight from nearly 8 million to over 21 million and women now accounted for about 43 per cent of the entire electorate. If women's voting qualifications had been made equal to those of British men they would have been in the majority because of the number of men of voting age lost in the war. It would take another decade for women to receive the same voting rights as men, however.

More locally things were looking up for the four parishes that now make up Castle Point. Development and the building of new infrastructure had slowed during the war, but as the economic depression of the 1920s faded, the parishes started to grow again. In 1930 Canvey at last built its bridge across to the mainland link.

Establishing War Memorials

A hundred years ago there were very few war memorials in Britain. Today there are thousands, largely due to this terrible conflict which was to change not only the political shape of the world, but also attitudes to war and the very nature of remembrance. People were determined not to forget the sacrifice made by those who lost their lives, so one by one war memorials were erected around the country.

These memorials ranged from simple stone tablets and plaques in chapels, through to monuments of all shapes and sizes in both town and country. They even encompassed entire buildings, including village halls and carvings on hillsides and dedicated tracts of land. The following section gives an overview of the various memorials established in our four south-east Essex parishes.

Canvey Island War Memorials:

Canvey Island War Memorial was erected in 1926, complete with a garden and a fountain, on the corner of Craven Avenue and Long Road (also known as Jones Corner). The land had been donated by George Chambers a well-known Canvey benefactor. For some reason the memorial was not unveiled until November 1932. It cost £200 and it was designed by Eugene Lawrence. There was a large gathering at the unveiling, which was carried out by Mrs George Woods, the mother of one of the local fallen.

Canvey Island Parish Memorial. (Photograph by Vic Russell)

The War Memorial in St Nicholas' Church, Canvey Island. (Photograph by Ken Porter, with kind permission of the church authorities)

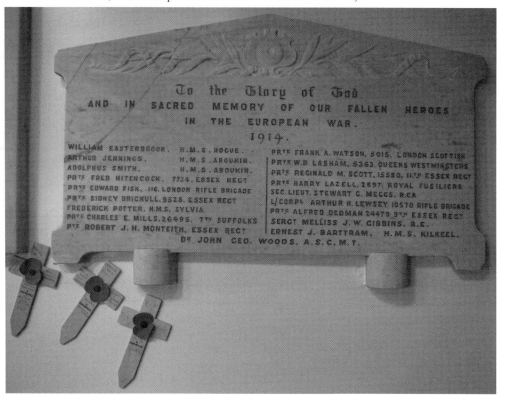

To the Glory of God
AND IN SACRED MEMORY OF OUR FALLEN HEROES
IN THE EUROPEAN WAR.
1914.

WILLIAM EASTERBROOK, H.M.S. HOGUE.
ARTHUR JENNINGS, H.M.S. ABOUKIR.
ADOLPHUS SMITH, H.M.S. ABOUKIR.
PRTE FRED HITCHCOCK, 7734. ESSEX REGT
PRTE EDWARD FISK, 116. LONDON RIFLE BRIGADE
PRTE SIDNEY BRIGNULL, 9528. ESSEX REGT
FREDERICK POTTER, H.M.S. SYLVIA
PRTE CHARLES E. MILLS, 26495, 7TH SUFFOLKS
PTE ROBERT J. H. MONTEITH, ESSEX REGT

PRTE FRANK A. WATSON, 5015, LONDON SCOTTISH
PRTE W.B LASHAM. 5363, QUEENS WESTMINSTERS
PRTE REGINALD M. SCOTT, 15580, 11TH ESSEX REGT
PRTE HARRY LAZELL, 2897, ROYAL FUSILIERS
SEC. LIEUT. STEWART G. MEGGS, R.F.A
L/CORPL ARTHUR H. LEWSEY 10570 RIFLE BRIGADE
PRTE ALFRED DEDMAN 24479 3TH ESSEX REGT
SERGT MELLISS J. W. GIBBINS, R.E.
ERNEST J. BARTTRAM, H.M.S. KILKEEL.

DR JOHN GEO. WOODS, A.S.C.M.T.

Robert Monteith war plaque in St Anne's Church, Canvey island. (Photograph by Ken Porter, with kind permission of Rev. Peter Mallinson)

Sometime in the 1950s, the war memorial was moved to the Paddocks and in March 1996 its plaque was presented to the Canvey Island branch of the British Legion, who attached it to the wall of their hall in Denham Road. It was eventually returned to the war memorial in time for Remembrance Day in 2010.

One mystery still not completely solved, is the story of the war memorial now in St Nicholas' Church, Canvey Island. It started out as one of the earliest church memorials in the country, as it was first erected in St Katherine's Church during 1915, but it includes only four names of local servicemen who had died in 1914: Easterbrook, Jennings, Smith and Hitchcock. It is uncertain whether subsequent war deaths were added as they were discovered or after the war had ended.

On Thursday, 21 January 2014, the *Basildon Evening Echo* reported that the Reverend Peter Mallinson of St Anne's Church, Canvey Island, had found three plaques buried beneath a shed in the garden of the church. It appears that they had been put there for safe-keeping when the old church was being demolished to make way for the new one.

One of the plaques belongs to Private Robert John Henry Monteith, a lay reader at the church, who and was killed on 6 September 1918. Robert enlisted at Southend on 9 October 1916 into the Essex Regiment, 9th Battalion. On 4 September 1918, the exhausted 9th Battalion relieved the 10th Battalion, then holding part of the line east of the Canal du Nord. This was followed the next day by a twenty-minute bombardment by the British, then the 9th with other battalions advanced in artillery formation. They incurred fierce retaliation from the enemy but, on reaching flat ground, they managed to hold firm until nightfall, when some some respite was gained.

On 6 September the 9th Battalion were able to advance, after negotiating two belts of wire but, in so doing, they sustained heavy casualties, Robert Monteith among them. However, the swiftness of their frontal attack caught the enemy by surprise, which enabled the capture of the 9th Battalion's objective.

Robert Monteith was awarded the Victory and British War Medals. He is buried at Fins New British Cemetery, Sorel-Le-Grand and is commemorated in addition to the plaque in St Anne's Church on the Canvey Island War Memorial.

Roll of Honour – Canvey Island:
- **Barttram, Ernest John** – Able Seaman, Royal Navy, HMS *Kilkeel* – died of pneumonia, 6 February 1919.
- **Brignull, Sidney** – Private, Essex Brigade, 1st Battalion – died 14 April 1917.
- **Dedman, Alfred** – Private, Essex Regiment, 9th Battalion – died 30 November 1917.
- **Easterbrook, William**– Able Seaman, Royal Navy, HMS *Hogue* – died 22 September 1914.
- **Fisk, Edward** – Private, London Rifle Brigade – died 27 April 1915.
- **Gibbins, Melliss Joseph William, (Military Medal)** – Sergeant, Royal Engineers, 79th Field Company – died 21 March 1918.

- **Hitchcock, Frederick** – Private, Essex Regiment, 2nd Battalion – died 28 December 1914.
- **Jennings, Arthur** – Royal Navy, HMS *Aboukir* – died 22 September 1914.
- **Lasham, William Baxter** – Private, 16th London Regiment, Queens Westminster Rifles – died 19 September 1916.
- **Lazell, Henry Edward** – Private, 11th Royal Fusiliers – died 4 November 1916.
- **Lewsey, Arthur Henry** – Lance Corporal, Machine Gun Corps (Infantry), 62nd Company – died 2 June 1917.
- **Meggs, Stewart Gordon** – Second Lieutenant, Royal Garrison Artillery Territorial Force – died 3 March 1917.
- **Mills, Charles E.**– Private, 6th Suffolk Regiment– died 18 August 1916.
- **Monteith, Robert J. H.** – Private, Essex Regiment, 9th Battalion – died 6 September 1918.
- **Potter, Frederick** – Able Seaman, Royal Navy – died 20 June 1917.
- **Scott, Reginald McLean** – Private, Machine Gun Corps, Essex Regiment, 11th Battalion – died 18 September 1916.
- **Smith, Adolphus Samuel** – Leading Signalman, Royal Navy, HMS *Aboukir* – died 22 September 1914.
- **Vallance, William** – Private, Bedford Regiment, 2nd Battalion – died 22 March 1918.
- **Watson, Frank Alexander** – Private, London Scottish – died 1 July 1916.
- **Woods, John George** – Driver, Royal Army Service Corps Mechanical Transport – died 22 December 1918.

South Benfleet War Memorial:
South Benfleet acted quickly to commemorate its war dead. The town's simple but impressive war memorial was unveiled on Sunday, 30 May 1920 by Colonel C.W. Collingwood CMG DS O RA, of Shoeburyness Garrison.

At the beginning of the ceremony the church choir sang the hymn 'Land of Hope and Glory', as they marched from the parish church. Colonel Collingwood made a short address, in which he said, 'That he was proud of the privilege accorded to him.' He then expressed his

The unveiling of the South Benfleet Parish War Memorial. (Contemporary photograph from the local paper)

admiration that a little village like South Benfleet should have sent so many men to the war; 25 per cent of whom had fallen. These men, he commented, had shown the spirit that had made England what she was. He then went on to say that those present, who were bereaved should be proud of those who had fallen and that there should not be any room for sorrow in their hearts.

Finally, he enlarged on the wonderful spirit of self-sacrifice and cheerfulness shown by all ranks in the war and expressed regret that the spirit of comradeship had not been maintained in commercial relations afterwards. He disapproved of what he called the 'great fuss' made of disabled and wounded men, as he considered that the ones who had really won the war were those who had given their lives. In conclusion, the Colonel expressed the certainty that those to whom he had just unveiled that memorial would never be forgotten by the people of South Benfleet and that their memory would be carried down from generation to generation.

The Vicar, Rev. A.C. Holthouse then dedicated the memorial and the Royal Field Artillery buglers from Shoeburyness Garrison played the 'Last Post' and 'Reveille'. The large crowd then sang the National Anthem and the choir as it returned to the church sang 'O God our Help in Ages Past.'

The site for the memorial opposite the local Post Office was donated by Mr T. Chambers. Sir Charles Nicholson designed the memorial and it was made by stone mason Percy Smith, funded by a public subscription. The seven-foot round square plinth is inscribed:

> *To the Glory of God. This memorial was erected by the parish of South Benfleet, in remembrance of those who fell in the Great War 1914-1918.*

On 28 February 2008 the memorial was designated Grade II listed. It still stands in its original position, but it is now opposite the Anchor Inn.

Roll of Honour – South Benfleet:
- **Alden, Arthur James** – Chief Petty Officer, Royal Navy, HMS *Partridge* – died 12 December 1917.
- **Arnup, Alex James** – Corporal, Lincolnshire Regiment, 10th Battalion – died 25 October 1918.

- **Anderson, James Edward** – Rifleman, Rifle Brigade, 12th Battalion – died 20 September 1917.
- **Box, Harold Francis** – Lieutenant, Essex Regiment, 5th Battalion Royal Engineers – died 29 October 1918.
- **Bright, Walter** – Driver, Royal Garrison Artillery, 125th Heavy Battery – died 2 January 1918.
- **Brittain, Percy James** – Private, London Regiment, 1st/24th Battalion – died 18 September 1916.
- **Brown, Charles James** – Private, Bedfordshire Regiment, 7th Battalion – died 14 August 1917.
- **Browne, Henry Arthur** – Second Lieutenant, Essex Regiment, 2nd Battalion – died 26 October 1918.
- **Burrells, William John** – Private, Essex Regiment, 2nd Battalion – died 10 October 1917.
- **Chiles, Stanley Moor** – Leading Seaman, Royal Navy, HMS *Aboukir* – died 22 September 1914.
- **Child, Robert Vivyan** – Private, East Surrey Regiment, 'B' Company 12th Battalion – died 15 September 1916.
- **Christie, H. H.** – Private, Suffolk Regiment, 2nd Battalion – died 9 June 1916.
- **Clarke, Ernest Albert** – Private, Northamptonshire Regiment, 2nd Battalion – died 24 August 1918.
- **Clement, Harold George** – Corporal 548, Royal Warwickshire Regiment, 16th Battalion – died 9 October 1917.
- **Clements, W. L.** – Sergeant, King's Royal Rifle Corps, 17th Battalion – died 3 September 1916.
- **Connor, Thomas** – Rifleman, London Regiment, 2nd/18th Battalion – died 23 December 1917.
- **Cowles, William Frederick** – Private, Essex Regiment, 'W' Company 1st Battalion – died 31 January 1918.
- **Ellison, Stanley Thomas** – Sapper, Royal Engineers, 56th Field Company – died 23 August 1914.
- **Farr, Albert G.** – Private, Essex Regiment, 9th Battalion – died 24 March 1917.
- **Farr, Frederick Edwin** – Private, Gloucestershire Regiment, 13th Battalion – died 22 March 1918.
- **Gerds, Frederick Niven** – Second Lieutenant, Royal Engineers, 176th Tunnelling Company – died 1 June 1915.

- **Gellard, Frank Charles–** Lance Corporal, East Lancashire Regiment, 6th Battalion – died 5 July 1916.
- **Gifford, John Leslie Patrick** – Corporal, Honourable Artillery Company, 2nd Battalion – died 11 March 1917.
- **Gladwin, William Charles** – Private, Australian Infantry AIF, 13th Battalion – died 29 August 1916.
- **Goodwin, W. T.** – Rifleman, London Regiment (Queen's Westminster Rifles), 16th Battalion – died 30 November 1917.
- **Gray, Harry** – Private, Northamptonshire Regiment, 1st Battalion – died 10 November 1917.
- **Gullet, James Antony** – Signal boy, Royal Navy, HMS *Black Prince* – died 31 May 1916.
- **Hine, John Thomas** – Private, Queen's Royal West Surrey Regiment, 6th Battalion – died 30 June   1918.
- **Jennings, John** – Lance Corporal, Essex Regiment, 2nd Battalion – died 13 May 1915.
- **Jennings, Ernest Albert** – Private, Essex Regiment, 1st Battalion – died 16 January 1916.
- **Jennings, Frederick** – Private, Queen's Own (Royal West Surrey Regiment) 11th Battalion – died 20 September 1917.
- **Kelsey, Henry Gordon** – Sergeant, Essex Regiment, 11th Battalion – died 2 July 1917.
- **King, Stanley Gordon** – Able Seaman, Royal Navy Volunteer Reserve, Hawke Battalion, Royal Navy Division – died 13 November 1916.
- **Lewsey, Arthur Henry** – Lance Corporal, Machine Gun Corps (Infantry), 62nd Company – died 2 June 1917.
- **Maclure, John** – Chief Steward, Mercantile Marine, SS *Mesaba* – died 1 September 1918.
- **Martin, W** – Private, 2nd Northampton Regiment – died 3 August 1916.
- **Meen, Harry Benjamin** – Private, King's Shropshire Light Infantry, 5th Battalion – died 18 March 1917.
- **Miles, Alfred Owen** – Private, Middlesex Regiment, 19th Battalion – died 6 February 1917.
- **Miller, Ernest Vivian** – Rifleman, London Regiment (London Irish Rifles), 1st/8th Battalion – died 25 September 1915.

- **Morrow, Horace Louis MM** – Corporal, Hampshire Regiment, 11th Battalion – died 21 November 1917.
- **Neville, Ernest George** – Private, Manchester Regiment, 2nd/7th Battalion – died 9 October 1917.
- **Newman, Herbert Henry** – Gunner, Royal Garrison Artillery, 390th Siege Battery – died 25 March 1919.
- **Odams, Walter Welford** – Private, Royal Fusiliers, 7th Battalion – died 17 July 1917.
- **Parry, George Frederick Arthur** – Corporal, Royal Garrison Artillery, 148th Siege Battery – died 25 December 1917.
- **Pearce, Charles Albert** – Private, The Queen's Royal West Surrey Regiment 10th Battalion – died 13 December 1916.
- **Peters, Albert William** – Private, Essex Regiment, 1st Battalion – died 23 April 1917.
- **Pilbrow, Stanley Smith** – Trooper, 2nd King Edward's Horse – died 9 December 1915.
- **Polley, Charles** – Gunner, Royal Garrison Artillery, 288th Siege Battery – died 4 August 1917.
- **Powell, John William** – Private, Middlesex Regiment, 12th Battalion 2nd Battalion 3rd County of Yeomany (Sharpshooters) – died 17 February 1917.
- **Revell, William James Ernest** – Private, Essex Yeomanry – died 28 September 1918.
- **Robinson, Ralf Hubert MM** – Second Lieutenant, Rifle Brigade, 2nd Battalion – died 23 August 1917.
- **Ross, George William** – Sub-Lieutenant, Royal Navy Volunteer Reserve, Howe Battalion, Royal Naval Division – died 4 June 1915.
- **Russell, Henry James** – Rifleman, King's Royal Rifle Corps, 2nd Battalion – died 9 September 1916.
- **Sargent, Samuel** – Private, York and Lancaster Regiment, 13th Battalion – died 12 April 1918.
- **Smith, Charles** – Mechanic, Royal Navy, HMS *Surprise* – died 23 December 1917.
- **Smith, Frank** – Rifleman, Rifle Brigade, 9th Battalion – died 30 July 1915.
- **Snow, Harry** – Private, Essex Regiment, 1st Battalion – died 8 May 1915.

- **St Leger, Dennis Claude Grant** – Second Lieutenant, Royal Field Artillery – died 22 March 1918.
- **Stevens, H.G.** – Private, Suffolk Regiment, 3rd Battalion – died 2 June 1919.
- **Stowers, Alfred Charley** – Private, York and Lancaster Regiment, 9th Battalion – died 12 January 1918.
- **Theobald, Samuel James** – Gunner, Royal Garrison Artillery, 288th Siege Battery – died 31 July 1917.
- **Thurtell, Charles Walter** – Lance Sergeant, Northamptonshire Regiment, 2nd Battalion – died 25 March 1918.
- **Tookey, Joseph Henry** – Private, Essex Regiment, 9th Battalion – died 19 October 1915.
- **Watson, Henry** – Private, Essex Regiment, 2nd Battalion – died 31 December 1916.
- **Weller, Archibald Arthur** – First Bed Steward, Mercantile marine, HMS *Llandovery Castle* – died 27 June 1918.
- **Weller, Reginald** – Private, Royal Fusiliers (City of London Regiment), 3rd Battalion – died 12 March 1915.
- **Whiteside, Reginald Cuthbert** – Sub-Lieutenant, Royal Flying Corps, 18th Squadron – died 20 December 1916.
- **Wilkin, Douglas Baker** – Private, Essex Regiment, 1st Battalion – died 23 August 1917.

Hadleigh War Memorial. (Postcard)

War Memorial, Hadleigh.

Hadleigh War Memorial today. (Photograph by Ken Porter, 2013)

Hadleigh War Memorial:

The *Chelmsford Chronicle* reported the unveiling of the Hadleigh War Memorial on 20 October 1922:

> *On Sunday afternoon close on 2,000 people assembled in and around the Recreation Ground at Hadleigh to witness the unveiling of the war memorial – an obelisk with stone steps and a square centre bearing the names of forty eight men who lost their lives in the war. Out of a total cost of £280 about £240 has been raised. The inscription on the monument, with the names of the men, is as follows:*
>
> *This monument was erected to the honour and undying memory of the men of this parish who laid down their lives for their King and Country in the Great War, 1914 – 1919.*
>
> *The men were very good and we were not hurt. They were a wall unto us, both by day and night.*
>
> *Lest we forget*

Mr A Hawkins presided at the impressive ceremony, which began with the National Anthem, played by the band of the Salvation Army from Hadleigh Colony – The Chairman said they were there to unveil a fitting emblem to their brave men who had died in the cause of liberty. It was an everlasting tribute to those brave fellows who had laid down their lives that others might live.

The hymn, 'O God, our help,' having been sung, Alderman J. H. Burrows, J.P., trusted that the names on that memorial would always be regarded with reverence and honour. He unveiled the memorial and the Rev. E. N. Gowing, R.D., dedicated it. – Mrs Burrows then came forward and laid the official wreath on the steps, followed by scores of people who covered the base with floral tributes.

Mr Munday, the Hon. Sec., then gave a report and read the names of the forty eight men. – The hymn, 'For all the Saints,' was followed by prayer by the Rev. E.M. Edmunds and then by the hymn. 'Abide with me,' after which the Benediction and 'The Last Post' and 'Reveille' closed the service.

Two weeks later, at the Parish Church, the Bishop of Barking dedicated a memorial shrine inscribed with the names of local men who had fallen in the war. It was designed by the Rev. D Adamson and stands in the church porch.

Roll of Honour – Hadleigh:
- **Allen, James Edward** – Corporal, Essex Regiment, 1st Battalion – died 8 April 1919.
- **Allen, Sidney Charles** – Acting Bombardier, Royal Garrison Artillery, Anti-Aircraft Dept – died 24 April 1918.
- **Arnold, John A.** – No reliable information.
- **Bartholomew, George Lee Walter** – 2nd Lieutenant, Royal Fusiliers – died 7 April 1918.
- **Burr, Harry Rivers** – Corporal, 2nd Royal Sussex Regiment – died 18 October 1918.
- **Bush, Herbert John** – Private, Essex Regiment, 2nd Battalion – died 15 October 1916.

THEIR NAME LIVETH FOR EVERMORE

1914	S.C.STAINES	T.FARLEY
H.J.WIFFEN	S.CHOPPEN	H.CLIFFORD
J.H.COOLLEDGE	H.MUNDAY	S.A.HAVES
1915	G.STIFF	(OF LEIGH)
J.H.COMPTON	C.F.WALLACE	C.J.W.LINCE
J.McCORMICK	J.RAYNER	E.MASON
H.SNOW	F.CARTER	F.W.SEWELL
W.STOKES	F.CHOPPEN	G.C.PIPER
A.WOODFORD	A.S.RAISON	C.TUCKER
A.GILBERT	H.J.BUSH	P.L.SMITH
C.EADE	R.FEAKIN	1918
H.G.SMITH	C.C.COLLINS	S.C.ALLEN
H.H.CALVERLEY	1917	J.A.ARNOLD
A.M.GINN	S.G.MEGGS	P.WHITE
J.STOCKWELL	R.MASON	J.W.UNDERWOOD
W.COWELL	D.SCOUGALL	R.COWELL
1916	R.COLLINS	1919
F.TUCKER	W.J.STAINES	J.E.ALLEN
S.G.PETCHEY	A.STAINES	

Memorial in Hadleigh Parish Church, St James the Less. (Photograph by Ken Porter 2013, with kind permission of the church authorities)

- **Calverley, Harold Henry** – Private, 12th Royal Fusiliers (City of London Regiment) – died 28 September 1915.
- **Carter, Frederick** – Private, Rifle Brigade (The Prince Consort's Own) 10th Battalion – died 3 September 1916. (Also appears on the Thundersley Church War Memorial.)
- **Choppen, Fred** – Rifleman, King's Royal Rifle Corps – died 15 September 1916. (Also appears on the Thundersley Church War Memorial.)
- **Choppen, Stephen** – Lance Corporal, Essex Regiment, 9th Battalion – died 25 May 1916.
- **Clarke, Frederick John** – Private, Essex Regiment – died 7 November 1919.
- **Clarke, John, Albert Arnold** – Private, 5th/7th Royal Sussex Regiment – died 26 April 1918.

William Cowell. (Postcard

- **Clifford, Harold** – Acting Sergeant, 11th Royal Sussex Regiment – died 18 September 1917.
- **Collins, Charles C**. – No reliable information.
- **Collins, Reginald** – Sergeant, 2nd/24th London Regiment – died 7 May 1917.
- **Compton, Jack Hugh** – Private 2nd Battalion East Surrey Regiment – died 25 April 1915.
- **Coolledge, John Henry** – Leading Stoker, Royal Fleet Reserve, HMS *Cressy* – died 22 September 1914.
- **Cowell, Richard** – Private, 25th Reserve Battalion of the Rifle Brigade/ 231st Labour Corps – died 19 November 1918.
- **Cowell, William** – Private, Essex Regiment, 9th Battalion – died 17 December 1915.
- **Dunn, Edwin Watson** – Sergeant, 2nd Suffolk Regiment – died 4 December 1914.
- **Eade, Charles** – Private, 2nd Bedfordshire Regiment – died 8 June 1915.
- **Farley, Thomas Henry** – Private, 1st Canadian Labour Corps – died 19 August 1917.

- **Feakin, Robert James** – Private, 7th King's Own Yorkshire Light Infantry – died 7 October 1916.
- **French, Jack** – Stoker, Royal Navy, HMS *Formidable* – died 1 January 1915.
- **Gilbert, Alfred** – Private, Essex Regiment, 1st Battalion – died 6 August 1915.
- **Ginn, Alfred** – Warrant Officer, Military Mounted Police – died 1 October 1915.
- **Hayes, Stanley Alfred** – Private, 13th Royal Sussex Regiment – died 26 September 1916.
- **Jemmett, Sidney Ernest** – Private, 4th East Kent Regiment (Buffs) – died 2 November 1918.
- **Lince, Charles William John** – Private, Duke of Cambridge's Own, 23rd Middlesex Regiment – died 29 September 1917.
- **Mason, Ernest Edward** – Private, Essex Regiment, 2nd Battalion – died 10 October 1917.
- **Mason, Reuben** – Private, 13th Hussars – died 5 March 1917.
- **McCormick, John Rowland** – Private, 3rd Royal Fusiliers – died 3 May 1915.
- **Meggs, Stewart Gordon** – 2nd Lieutenant, Royal Garrison Artillery, 213th Siege Battalion – died 3 March 1917. Also appears on the Thundersley Church War Memorial.
- **Munday, Henry** – Corporal, 1st East Yorkshire Regiment – died 1 July 1916.
- **Petchey, Sidney George** – Lance Corporal, Essex Regiment, 9th Battalion – died 2 April 1916.
- **Piper, William George** – Private, Essex Regiment, 5th Battalion – died 2 November 1917.
- **Raison, Arthur Stanley** – Private, 32nd Royal Fusiliers – died 19 September 1917.
- **Rayner, Joseph** – Private, 18th Northamptonshire Regiment – died 18 August 1916.
- **Scougall, Douglas Muir** – 2nd Lieutenant, 1st/15th London Regiment (Rifle Brigade) – died 4 May 1917.
- **Sewell, Frederick William** – Private, 1st South Staffordshire Regiment – died 26 October 1917.
- **Smith, Harold George** – Acting Quartermaster, Royal Naval Reserve, HMS *India* – died 8 August 1915.

- **Smith, Percy Louis** – Airman (Second Class), Royal Flying Corps, 111th Squadron – died 3 December 1917.
- **Snow, Henry** – Private, Essex Regiment, 1st Battalion – died 8 May 1915.
- **Staines, Archie** – Bombardier, Royal Garrison Artillery – died 14 August 1917.
- **Staines, Sidney Charles** – Private, 5th Coldstream Guards – died 16 April 1916.
- **Staines, Wilfred James** – Corporal, 9th Royal Fusiliers (City of London Regiment) – died 23 June 1917.
- **Stiff, George** – Private, Essex Regiment, 10th Battalion – died 20 July 1916.
- **Stockwell, James** – Private, 2nd Royal Fusiliers (City of London Regiment) – died 14 November 1915.
- **Stokes, William** – Private, 2nd Leicestershire Regiment – died 15 May 1915.
- **Tucker, Cecil** – Private, 17th Royal Fusiliers – died 28 November 1917.
- **Tucker, Frederick John** – Private, 1st Border Regiment – died 28 November 1917.
- **Underwood, John William** – Private, 9th Royal Fusiliers – died 28 August 1918.

- **Wallace, Charles Frederick** – Canadian Infantry (British Columbia regiment) 29th Vancouver Battalion – died 22 July 1916.
- **White, Philip** – Acting Sergeant Essex Regiment, 1st Battalion – died 8 November 1915.
- **Wiffen, Harry John** – Corporal, 56th Field Company, Royal Engineers – died 23 August 1914.
- **Woodford, Alfred** – Private, Essex Regiment, 1st Battalion – died 22 June 1915.

Thundersley Church War Memorial:
Unlike the other three parishes, Thundersley does not have a village war memorial and therefore relies on the war memorial in the local parish church. From notes written by Reverend E. Maley, who was the Rector from 1916 to the early 1950s, the bronze First World War Memorial was presented to St Peter's Church by Mr Sheridan, Mr Scopes and Mr Veness.

Roll of Honour – Thundersley:
- **Aldridge, Leslie** – Lance Corporal, Rifle Brigade, 3rd Battalion – died 22 March 1918.
- **Bashford, W.W.G. MM**– Sergeant, Essex Regiment, 9th Battalion – died 17 July 1917.
- **Bone, W.J.A.** – Private, Essex Regiment, 6th Battalion – died 3 October 1915.
- **Boosey, Thomas Frank** – Private, Royal Fusiliers, 9th Battalion – died 7 July 1916.
- **Carter, Frederick** – Private, Rifle Brigade (The Prince Consort's Own), 10th Battalion – died 3 September 1916. (Also appears on the Hadleigh War Memorial.)
- **Carter, Charles Ernest** – Private, 1st Royal Munster Fusiliers – died 21 August 1917.
- **Choppen, Fred** – Rifleman, King's Royal Rifle Corps – died 15 September 1916. (Also appears on the Hadleigh War Memorial.)
- **Clark, Frank** – Private, Machine Gun Corps – died 10 December 1918.
- **Davis, Hubert** – Private, 5th Suffolk Regiment – died 1 June 1917.

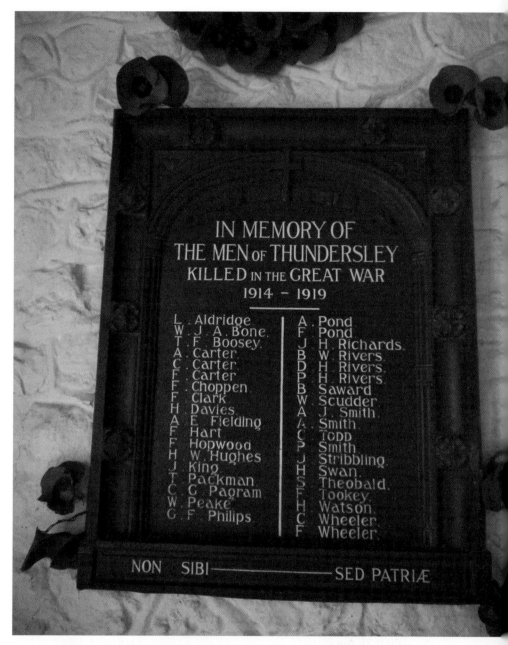

Memorial in St Peter's Parish Church, Thundersley. (Photograph by Ken Porter 2013, with kind permission of of the church authorities)

- **Ellison, Stanley** – Sapper, Royal Engineers, 56th Company – died 23 August 1914.
- **Fielding, Albert Edward** – Private, Essex Regiment, 10th Battalion – died 2 November 1917.
- **Gullett, James Anthony** – First Class Signaller, Royal Navy, HMS *Black Prince* – died 31 May 1916.
- **Hand, George Charles** – Australian Imperial Force – died 3 December 1916.
- **Hart, Frederick** – First Class Stoker, Royal Navy HMS *Queen Mary* – died 31 May 1916.
- **Hopwood, Frederick William MM** – Second Lieutenant, 5th Royal Berkshire Regiment – died 27 August 1918.
- **Hughes, Hugh William** – Private, 143rd Canadian Contingent – died 17 September 1917.
- **King, Herbert John** – Lance Corporal, Essex Regiment, 2nd Battalion – died 21 May 1917.
- **Meggs, Stewart Gordon** – Second Lieutenant, Royal Garrison Artillery – died 2 March 1917. (Also appears on the Hadleigh War Memorial.)
- **Monk, Ernest James** – Private, Labour Corps – died 20 February 1919.
- **Pagram, Claud Ganville** – Private, 3rd Royal Fusiliers – died 8 May 1915.
- **Philips, George Frederick** – Signaller, Royal Field Artillery – died 17 April 1917.
- **Peake, William Hadwen** – Private, 24th Royal Fusiliers (City of London) Sportsman's Battalion – died 31 July 1916.
- **Pond, Arthur Edward** – Lance Corporal, Essex Regiment, 9th Battalion – died 13 October 1915.
- **Pond, Frederick Charles** – Rifleman, Kings Royal Rifle Corps – died 10 November 1917.
- **Richards, J. H.** – Gunner, Royal Field Artillery – died 24 April 1918.
- **Sargent, Samuel** – Private, 13th Yorkshire and Lancashire Regiment – died 12 April 1918.
- **Saward, Bert Louis** – Private, 6th Royal West Kent Regiment – died 28 April 1917.

- **Scudder, William** – Private, 2nd Grenadier Guards – died 27 August 1918.
- **Smith, E.A.** – Private, South Wales Borders – died 4 June 1917.
- **Smith, Percy Louis** – Percy Louis, Second Class Air Mechanic RAF – died 2 December 1917.
- **Swann, Henry George** – Private, Essex Regiment, 2nd Battalion – died 21 November 1914.
- **Theobald, Samuel** – Gunner, Royal Garrison Artillery – died 31 July 1917.
- **Todd, Jack** – Lance Corporal, Loyal North Lancashire Regiment – died 11 April 1917.
- **Tookey, Ferdinand Sidney** – Private, 2nd/4th Berkshire Regiment – died 31 August 1918.
- **Watson, Henry** – Private, Essex Regiment, 2nd Battalion – died 31 December 1918.
- **White Philip** – Sergeant, Essex Regiment, 1st Battalion – died 8 November 1918.
- **Withers, G. F.** – Acting Corporal, King's Royal Rifle Corps – died 6 December 1917.

The following are individuals appearing on the Thundersley Church Memorial about whom the authors have not been able to find any information: A. Carter, T. Packman, B. W. Rivers, D. H. Rivers, P. H. Rivers, A. J. Smith, J. Stribbling, C. Wheeler, F. Wheeler.

Not all of the names listed above appeared on the local parishes or church war memorials, possibly because their families had moved out of the area and in some cases individuals appear on more than one of the four parish memorials. Of the 16,000 villages and towns that existed in Britain in 1914, fifty-five 'Thankful Villages' saw all their servicemen return home and fourteen of those fifty-five would see all of their servicemen return home after the Second World War as well.

Remembrance Day

Every year on 11 November at 11.00am, the people of all Commonwealth countries commemorate members of the armed forces who died in the line of duty during the First World War and a two-minute silence is observed. The very first Remembrance Day was held in the grounds of Buckingham Palace on the morning of 11 November 1919.

To many, this occasion is also known as Armistice Day or Poppy Day. The red poppy has become the familiar emblem of Remembrance Day, due to the poem 'In Flanders Fields' by Lieutenant Colonel John McCrae.

> *In Flanders fields the poppies blow*
> *Between the crosses, row on row,*
> *That mark our place and in the sky*
> *The larks, still bravely singing, fly*
> *Scarce heard amid the guns below.*
> *We are Dead, short days ago*
> *We lived, felt dawn, saw sunset glow,*
> *Loved and were loved and now we lie*
> *In Flanders Fields.*
>
> *Take up our quarrel with the foe*
> *To you from failing hands we throw*
> *The torch; be yours to hold it high.*
> *If we break faith with us who die*
> *We shall not sleep, though poppies grow*
> *In Flanders fields.*

The First World War has almost deserted living memory, so why has it become so firmly rooted in the modern mind? The Second World War is rightly prominent too, but there are still surviving veterans to remind us of their experiences. Yet the Boer Wars, which ended in 1902, have been virtually forgotten.

Part of the reason behind our continuing fascination with the 1914-1918 war must be because of the sheer scale of the slaughter and on the centenary of this war, its memory grows stronger and stronger. More than 300,000 people each year still visit the battlefields of Northern France and many more visit the Menin Gate at Ypres at 8.00pm every evening and hear the buglers play the 'Last Post', which has been played uninterrupted since 2 July 1918, except during the Second World War when the area was occupied by German troops. The daily service was then conducted at Brookwood Military Cemetery in Surrey, instead.

Over the past few years we have seen the last of the surviving veterans from this war pass away, but unlike previous wars, as has been said many times before, this war must not be forgotten. It marked the beginning of the modern age and its shock waves are still being felt today within our political and social structures and within our economy and technology.

Finally, the 'Ode of Remembrance' taken from Laurence Binyon's poem, 'For the Fallen':

> *They shall grow not old, as we that are left grow old;*
> *Age shall not weary them, nor the years condemn.*
> *At the going down of sun and in the morning*
> *We will remember them.*

Sources

Contemporary publications:
Chelmsford Chronicle
Essex Newsman
Kelly's Directories
Southend Standard
This England magazine (Spring 1914)

Books:
Adams, Simon, *Eyewitness World War 1* (Dorling Kindersley, 2004)
Balcon, Jill, *The Pity of War – Poems of the First World War*
    (Shepheard-Walwyn Ltd, 1985)
Beckett, R.A. *Romantic Essex* (PBK Publishing, 2001)
Buchan, Robert, *Andromeda* (1900)
Chisman, Norman M., *Bygone Benfleet* (Phillimore, 1991)
Hallmann, Robert, *Canvey Island, a History* (Phillimore, 2006)
Hancock, M.; Harvey, S., *Hadleigh* (Phillimore, 1986)
Jarvis, Jeffrey, *Southend Roll of Honour 1914-1921* (Compiled from
    original sources, 1998)
McCave, Fred, *A History of Canvey Island* (Ian Henry Publications,
    1985)
Parkhill, Gordon; Cook, Graham, *Hadleigh Salvation Army Farm: A
    Vision Reborn* (Salvation Army, 2008)
Priestley, H. E.; Phillips, Wyn T., *History of Benfleet Book Two*
    (Privately printed).
Rusiecki, Paul, *The Impact of Catastrophe: The People of Essex and
    the First World War (1914-1920)* (Essex Record Office, 2008)
Western Front Association, Essex Branch, *Men of Essex Series*
    (various titles)
Westwell, Ian, *World War 1 Day by Day* (Grange Books, 2000)

Websites:
Ancestry.co.uk: *www.ancestry.co.uk*
Commonwealth War Graves Commission: *www.cwgs.org*
Essex Record Office (Seax): *www.seax.essexcc.gov.uk*
Findmypast.co.uk: *www.findmypast.co.uk*
First World War.com: *www.firstworldwar.com*
Forces War Records: *www.forces-war-records*
The National Archives: *www.nationalarchives.gov.uk*
The Wartime Memories Project: *www.wartimememories.co.uk*

Index